Chocolate Ecstasy

CHOCOLATE ECSTASY

75 of the most dangerous recipes ever

CHRISTINE FRANCE

INDEX

First published by Lorenz Books in 1996

© 1996 Anness Publishing Limited

**Lorenz Books is an imprint of
Anness Publishing Limited
Hermes House, 88-89 Blackfriars Road
London SE1 8HA**

This edition distributed in Canada by Raincoast Books Distribution Limited

ISBN 1 85967 204 3

A CIP catalogue record for this book
is available from the British Library

Publisher: Joanna Lorenz
Senior Cookery Editor: Linda Fraser
Cookery Editor: Rosemary Wilkinson
Copy Editor: Jenni Fleetwood
Designer: Annie Moss
Mac Artist: John Fowler
Photography: Steve Baxter
Food for Photography: Jane Stevenson
Styling: Diana Civil

Printed and bound in Hong Kong

3 5 7 9 10 8 6 4 2

NOTES
For all recipes, quantities are given in both metric and imperial measures and, where appropriate, measures
are also given in standard cups and spoons.
Follow one set, but not a mixture because they are not interchangeable.

Standard spoon and cup measurements are level.
1 tsp = 5ml, 1 tbsp = 15ml, 1 cup = 250ml/8fl oz

Australian standard tablespoons are 20ml. Australian readers should use 3 tsp in place of 1 tbsp for
measuring small quantities of gelatine, cornflour, salt etc.

Size 3 (medium) eggs should be used unless otherwise stated.

$\mathscr{C}$ONTENTS

$\mathcal{I}$NTRODUCTION

Few foods are as rich, sensuous and wickedly
tempting as chocolate. Whether you nibble it,
savour it or simply surrender to its charms,
chocolate is pure pleasure. There's something
almost addictive about this gift of the gods, as
anyone who has ever tried to give it up,
however briefly, will testify.

*T*he ultimate decadent treat, it is hardly surprising that in the past chocolate has been credited with being an aphrodisiac. Chocolates are traditional lovers' gifts, and special events, such as Easter and Christmas, are celebrated with chocolate eggs or the traditional yuletide log.

Once the preserve of Aztec emperors, highly prized and coveted, chocolate was unknown in Europe until the middle of the 16th century, when it was introduced as a rare and wonderful beverage. It took almost two hundred years before the sweetened chocolate bar made its appearance, and the rest, as they say, is history. Although chocolate is now accessible to all, familiarity has done nothing to dim its popularity. Consumption of all types of chocolate continues to rise. In recent years there has been an increased demand for the pure product with more than 50 per cent cocoa solids, and foodies scout out new varieties of chocolate with all the enthusiasm and energy of the ardent wine buff or truffle fancier.

For the cook, the fascination with chocolate goes even deeper. It is a sensitive ingredient which needs careful handling, but which offers remarkable rewards. The velvety texture and rich flavour add a touch of luxury to numerous cakes, cookies, puddings and desserts, and it is equally good in hot or cold dishes.

As an added bonus, chocolate can be piped, shaped and moulded to make a variety of exciting decorations. Full instructions, with detailed advice on a range of other techniques, are included in the introduction.

This is a book for serious chocolate lovers. As you would expect, we've included classics like Black Forest Gâteau and Double Chocolate Chip Muffins, but — and this is the mark of the true chocoholic — we've also investigated every conceivable way of introducing our favourite ingredient into familiar and much-loved dishes. There's a rich chocolate trifle, a rare chocolate pavlova (with

cocoa giving the meringue a dusky appearance and delectable flavour), an unusual chocolate crème brûlée, a chocolate zabaglione and even a chocolate and cherry polenta cake.

Basic advice includes instructions for making chocolate pastry, and for those who really don't believe you can get too much of a good thing, there are double delights like Tiramisu in Chocolate Cups, White Chocolate Vanilla Mousse with Dark Chocolate Sauce and Steamed Chocolate and Fruit Puddings with Chocolate Syrup.

Also in the luscious line-up are crunchy chocolate chip cookies, chocolate sponge cakes with fudgy centres, gloriously gooey puddings, voluptuous gâteaux and sweet chocolate treats for gifts and after-dinner delights. In honour of those ancient Aztecs, there's a recipe for Mexican Hot Chocolate and even an iced chocolate and peppermint drink.

So go on — indulge yourself. But take it slow and easy — Death by Chocolate could be just around the corner!

Types of Chocolate

COUVERTURE

The professionals' choice, this is a fine quality pure chocolate with a high percentage of cocoa butter, which gives it a high gloss. It is suitable for decorative use and for making handmade chocolates. Couverture is expensive and must generally be tempered before use (see page 13). Specialist chocolate shops sell couverture chocolate.

PLAIN DARK CHOCOLATE

Often called "luxury", "bitter" or "continental" chocolate, this has a high percentage of cocoa solids – around 75% – with little or no added sugar. Many people find plain dark chocolate too bitter for eating, but its rich, intense flavour and good dark colour make it an ideal ingredient in desserts or cakes.

PLAIN CHOCOLATE

Ordinary plain chocolate is the most widely available chocolate to use in cooking. It contains anywhere between 30% and 70% cocoa solids, so check the label before you buy. The higher the cocoa solids, the better the chocolate flavour will be.

MILK CHOCOLATE

This contains powdered or condensed milk and generally has around 20% cocoa solids. The flavour is mild and sweet. Although this is the most popular eating chocolate, it is not as suitable as plain chocolate for melting and cooking.

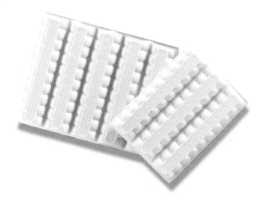

WHITE CHOCOLATE

This does not contain any cocoa solids, but gets its flavour from cocoa butter. It is sweet, and the better quality white chocolate is quite rich and smooth. White chocolate must be melted with care as it does not withstand heat as well as plain chocolate and is liable to stiffen if allowed to get too hot.

CHOCOLATE CHIPS

These are small pieces of chocolate of uniform size, convenient for stirring directly into biscuit dough or cake mixture, or for melting. They contain fewer cocoa solids than ordinary chocolate, and are available in plain dark, plain, milk and white.

COCOA

This is made from the pure cocoa mass after most of the cocoa butter has been extracted. The mass is roasted, then ground to make a powder. It is probably the most economical way of giving puddings and baked goods a chocolate flavour.

ORGANIC CHOCOLATE

This is slightly more expensive than other types of chocolate but is a quality product, high in cocoa solids, produced without pesticides and with consideration for the environment. Dark, milk and flavoured varieties are available.

CHOCOLATE-FLAVOUR CAKE COVERING

This is a blend of sugar, vegetable oil, cocoa and flavourings. As its name suggests, it should only be used for covering or decoration as the flavour is poor. However, the high fat content makes it suitable for making chocolate curls or caraque – to improve the flavour, melt a few squares with good plain chocolate.

TECHNIQUES

Melting Chocolate

There are basically three ways to melt chocolate:

USING A DOUBLE BOILER

1 Fill the base of a double boiler or saucepan about a quarter full. Fit the top pan or place a heatproof bowl over the saucepan. The water should not touch the top container. Bring the water to just below boiling point, then turn down the heat to the lowest possible setting.

2 Break the chocolate into squares and place in the top pan or bowl. Leave to melt completely, without stirring. Keep the water at a very slow simmer.

TIPS FOR MELTING CHOCOLATE

• Melt chocolate slowly, as overheating will spoil both the flavour and texture.
• Avoid overheating – dark chocolate should not be heated above 49°C/120°F; milk and white chocolate should not go above 43°C/110°F.
• Never allow water or steam to come into contact with melting chocolate, as this may cause it to stiffen.
• Do not cover chocolate after melting, as condensation could cause it to stiffen.

MELTING IN THE MICROWAVE

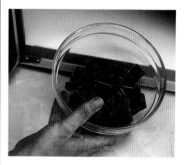

Break the chocolate into squares and place it in a bowl suitable for use in the microwave. Heat until just softened – chocolate burns easily in the microwave, so check often, remembering that chocolate retains its shape when melted in this way.

Approximate times for melting plain or milk chocolate in a 650-700 watt microwave oven:

115g/4oz	2 minutes on High (100% power)
200-225g/7-8oz	3 minutes on High (100% power)
115g/4oz white chocolate	2 minutes on Medium (50% power)

DIRECT HEAT METHOD

This is only suitable for recipes where the chocolate is melted in plenty of other liquid, such as milk or cream. Break up the chocolate into a saucepan. Add the liquid, then heat gently, stirring occasionally, until the chocolate has melted and the mixture is smooth.

Storing Chocolate

Chocolate keeps well if stored in a cool, dry place, away from strong smelling foods. Check "best before" dates on the pack.

Tempering Chocolate

Couverture (pure chocolate with no fats other than cocoa butter) must be tempered before use to distribute the cocoa fat evenly and produce a glossy finish. It is useful for special decorations or for moulded chocolates.

1 Break up the chocolate into small pieces and place it in the top of a double boiler or a heatproof bowl over a saucepan of hot water. Heat gently until just melted.

2 Tip about three-quarters of the chocolate on to a marble slab or a cool, smooth work surface.

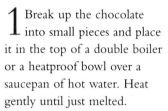

3 With a flexible plastic scraper or palette knife, spread the chocolate thinly, then scoop it up, keeping it constantly on the move, for about 5 minutes.

4 Using a chocolate thermometer, check the temperature of the chocolate as you work it. As soon as the temperature registers 28°C/82°F, tip the chocolate back into the bowl and stir into the remaining chocolate.

5 With the addition of the hot chocolate, the temperature should now be 32°C/90°F, and the chocolate is ready for use. To test, drop a little of the chocolate from a spoon on to the marble; it should set very quickly.

Chocolate Decorations

All these decorations can be made using plain, milk or white chocolate.

GRATED CHOCOLATE

Using a fine or coarse cheese grater or the grating blade of a food processor, grate a large bar of chocolate. Grated chocolate is useful for sprinkling over desserts or cakes, or coating the sides of gâteaux. If you use a cheese grater, stand it on a sheet of non-stick baking paper for extra convenience. The grated chocolate can then be easily tipped or brushed off as required.

QUICK CHOCOLATE CURLS

Use a swivel bladed vegetable peeler to shave curls of chocolate from the whole bar. This works best when the chocolate has been brought to room temperature.

CHOCOLATE CURLS

This method makes larger chocolate curls.

1 Spread melted chocolate thinly and evenly over a marble slab or a cool, smooth work surface. Leave until it is just set.

2 Push a metal scraper or cheese slicer across the surface, at a 25° angle, to remove thin shavings of chocolate which should curl gently against the blade. If the chocolate sets too hard it may become too brittle to curl and must be gently melted again.

CARAQUE

This method makes beautiful, long, curled shavings which are a really special decoration for gâteaux and desserts. To make marbled caraque, spread out dark and white chocolate in stripes.

1 Spread melted chocolate thinly and evenly over a marble slab or a cool, smooth work surface. Leave until it is just set.

2 Using a cook's knife with a straight, rigid blade, pull the blade across the surface of the chocolate at an angle of about 45°, to remove fine, curled shavings.

PIPED SHAPES

Use your imagination when piping shapes, from simple swirls or zigzags to intricate flowers or initials, to decorate that special cake.

1 Spoon about 15ml/1 tbsp of melted chocolate into a small paper piping bag. Secure the top and snip a small amount from the tip of the bag with scissors.

2 Spread a sheet of non-stick baking paper on a cool, smooth work surface or inverted baking sheet. Draw shapes on the paper as a guide if you like, or work freehand.

3 Leave the outlines as they are or fill them in to make solid decorations (a contrasting colour of chocolate looks very effective). Leave until set before carefully lifting the shapes off the paper.

4 To make curved shapes, place the paper over a rolling pin or similar shape when drying the chocolate.

CUT-OUTS

Simple cut-out shapes are a useful decoration for all kinds of cakes and desserts. Dark and white chocolate can be marbled together for a special effect.

1 Melt the chocolate and spread it on a sheet of non-stick baking paper. Leave until just set.

2 Use a sharp knife to cut triangles or squares from the chocolate, or stamp out decorative shapes, such as hearts and flowers.

CHOCOLATE LEAVES

Use any non-poisonous fresh leaves, such as rose, mint, bay, strawberry or lemon geranium. The leaves should be clean, dry and unblemished. Use both dark and white chocolate to make variegated leaves.

1 Melt the chocolate and use a small paintbrush to paint over the underside of each leaf, just up to the edges. The chocolate coating should be even and not too thin, or it will crack when you remove it.

2 Lay the leaves, chocolate side up, on a sheet of non-stick baking paper and leave to set completely.

3 When the chocolate has set, carefully peel away the leaves to reveal the veined chocolate leaves. If necessary, pack into airtight boxes and store in a cool place.

FEATHERED OR MARBLED CHOCOLATE

These two related techniques provide some of the easiest and most effective ways of decorating the top of a cake, and are also used when making a swirled mixture for cut-outs. Chocolate sauce and double cream can also be feathered or marbled to decorate a dessert.

1 Melt two contrasting colours of chocolate and spread one over the cake or surface to be used.

2 Spoon the contrasting chocolate into a piping bag and pipe lines or swirls over the chocolate.

3 Working quickly before the chocolate sets, draw a skewer or cocktail stick through the swirls to create a feathered or marbled effect.

CHOCOLATE RIBBONS

These look particularly effective if dark and white chocolate are used together, in stripes, dots or marbled.

1 Cut strips of clear acetate into long, thin strips, about 15 x 5cm/6 x 2in.

2 Melt the chocolate and spoon into piping bags. Pipe the chocolate in your chosen design over the strips, making a straight edge. Use a ruler to guide your hand in a straight line.

3 Allow to cool until it holds its shape but do not allow it to set. Bend each ribbon over with the acetate and secure with tape. Leave until completely set, then peel away the acetate.

$\mathcal{E}$QUIPMENT

Working with chocolate requires little by way of special equipment. Most items will be found in any well-stocked kitchen, but you may need to buy one or two extra pieces of equipment if you plan to mould chocolates.

CHEESE SLICER
The blade is drawn across a thin layer of just-set chocolate to make curls or caraque.

CHOCOLATE MOULDS
Most small chocolate moulds are made from flexible plastic, though some larger ones, such as Easter egg moulds, are made from polished metal.

CHOCOLATE THERMOMETER
Mainly used for tempering chocolate, this is a specialist item.

CHOCOLATE TOOLS
Professionals use these for dipping and marking chocolates. Buy them from specialist cake decorating suppliers.

COCKTAIL STICKS AND SKEWERS
These are useful for marbling chocolate and moving delicate shapes such as caraque or curls.

DECORATIVE CUTTERS
Small biscuit or aspic cutters are handy for making decorative shapes from thin sheets of set chocolate.

DOUBLE BOILER
This is useful for melting chocolate over simmering water, but a heatproof bowl fitted over an ordinary saucepan can be used instead, if done carefully.

FLEXIBLE SCRAPER
This is an asset when making chocolate caraque and shavings.

KNIVES
Small sharp knives are required for cutting chocolate shapes, while a large cook's knife with a rigid non-serrated blade is necessary for making caraque.

MARBLE SLAB
Although not essential, this provides a cold, flat surface for spreading chocolate to make caraque or shapes, and is also used when tempering chocolate. A clean work surface or an inverted baking sheet can be used instead.

MIXING BOWLS
A selection of mixing bowls in various sizes is essential. Heatproof bowls are necessary for melting chocolate, and a large glass or ceramic bowl will be invaluable for whisking egg whites.

PAINTBRUSHES
Small paintbrushes can be used for spreading chocolate thinly over leaves or inside moulds. Choose good quality brushes which will not shed hairs.

PALETTE KNIFE
This is the perfect tool for spreading melted chocolate or frostings.

SIEVE
A standard sieve is needed for sifting cocoa and icing sugar. For very small quantities, use a tea strainer.

VEGETABLE PEELER
Use this for making chocolate curls.

1. DOUBLE BOILER

2. KNIFE

3. PALETTE KNIFE

4. FLEXIBLE SCRAPER

5. CHEESE SLICER

6. VEGETABLE PEELER

7. CHOCOLATE TOOLS

8. CHOCOLATE THERMOMETER

9. PAINTBRUSHES

10. COCKTAIL STICKS AND SKEWERS

11. CHOCOLATE MOULDS

12. DECORATIVE CUTTERS

13. SIEVE

14. MIXING BOWLS

15. MARBLE SLAB

$\mathcal{S}$MALL CAKES AND BAKES

There's no end to the ways to use chocolate in
small cakes and cookies. Start the day with a
warm Brioche au Chocolat for breakfast,
or treat yourself at coffee time with rich,
totally indulgent Nut and Chocolate Chip
Brownies or Double Chocolate Chip Muffins.
Or, if you're after an elegant touch of texture
to serve alongside a creamy dinner party
dessert, light, crisp Chocolate Cinnamon
Tuiles are the perfect choice.

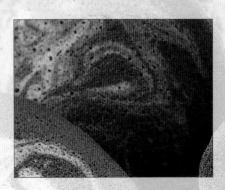

NUT AND CHOCOLATE CHIP BROWNIES

INGREDIENTS

150g/5oz plain chocolate, broken into squares

120ml/4fl oz/½ cup sunflower oil

215g/7½oz/1¼ cups light muscovado sugar

2 eggs

5ml/1 tsp vanilla essence

65g/2½oz/⅔ cup self-raising flour

60ml/4 tbsp cocoa powder

75g/3oz/¾ cup chopped walnuts or pecan nuts

60ml/4 tbsp milk chocolate chips

~ MAKES 16 ~

> *Moist, dark and deeply satisfying –*
> *meet the ultimate chocolate brownie.*

1 Preheat the oven to
~ 180°C/350°F/Gas 4.
Lightly grease a shallow
19cm/7½in square cake tin.
Melt the plain chocolate in a
heatproof bowl over hot water.

COOK'S TIP

These brownies will
freeze for 3 months in an
airtight container

2 Beat the oil, sugar, eggs
~ and vanilla essence together
in a large bowl.

3 Stir in the melted
~ chocolate, then beat well
until evenly mixed.

4 Sift the flour and cocoa
~ powder into the bowl and
fold in thoroughly.

5 Stir in the chopped nuts
~ and chocolate chips, tip
into the prepared tin and
spread evenly to the edges.

6 Bake for 30-35 minutes, or
~ until the top is firm and
crusty. Cool in the tin before
cutting into squares.

WHITE CHOCOLATE MACADAMIA SLICES

Keep these luxury slices for someone special who'll really appreciate their superb rich flavour and crunchy texture.

1 Preheat the oven to 190°C/375°F/Gas 5. Lightly grease two 20cm/8in round sandwich cake tins and line the base of each with greaseproof or non-stick baking paper.

2 Roughly chop the nuts and half the white chocolate, making sure that the pieces are more or less the same size, then cut up the apricots to similar size pieces.

3 In the top of a double boiler or a heatproof bowl over barely simmering water, melt the remaining white chocolate with the butter. Remove from the heat and stir in the vanilla essence.

4 Whisk the eggs and sugar together in a mixing bowl until thick and pale, then pour in the melted chocolate mixture, whisking constantly.

5 Sift the flour over the mixture and fold it in evenly. Finally, stir in the nuts, chopped white chocolate and chopped dried apricots.

6 Spoon into the tin and level the top. Bake for 30–35 minutes, or until the top is firm and crusty. Cool in the tin before cutting into squares.

COOK'S TIP

Use kitchen scissors to snip the apricots into small pieces.

CHOCOLATE CINNAMON TUILES

Slim, curvy and quite irresistible, tuiles are the perfect accompaniment for sophisticated desserts.

INGREDIENTS

1 egg white

50g/2oz/¼ cup caster sugar

30ml/2 tbsp plain flour

40g/1½oz/3 tbsp butter, melted

15ml/1 tbsp cocoa powder

2.5ml/½ tsp ground cinnamon

⇝ MAKES 12 ⇜

1 Preheat the oven to 200°C/400°F/Gas 6. Lightly grease two large baking sheets. Whisk the egg white in a clean, grease-free bowl until it forms soft peaks. Gradually whisk in the sugar to make a smooth, glossy mixture.

COOK'S TIP

Work as quickly as possible when removing the tuiles from the baking sheets – if they firm up too quickly, pop the baking sheet back in the oven for a minute and try again.

2 Sift the flour over the mixture and fold in evenly. Stir in the butter. Transfer about 45ml/3 tbsp of the mixture to a small bowl and set it aside.

3 In a separate bowl, mix together the cocoa and cinnamon. Stir into the larger quantity of mixture.

4 Leaving room for spreading, drop spoonfuls of the chocolate-flavoured mixture on to the prepared baking sheets, then spread each gently with a palette knife to make a neat round.

5 Using a small spoon, drizzle the reserved plain mixture over the rounds, swirling it lightly to give a marbled effect.

6 Bake for 4-6 minutes, until just set. Using a palette knife, lift each biscuit carefully and quickly drape it over a rolling pin, to give a curved shape as it hardens.

7 Allow the tuiles to cool until set, then remove them gently and finish cooling on a wire rack. Serve on the same day.

DOUBLE CHOCOLATE CHIP MUFFINS

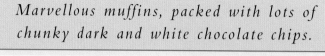

> *Marvellous muffins, packed with lots of chunky dark and white chocolate chips.*

INGREDIENTS

400g/14oz/3½ cups plain flour

15ml/1 tbsp baking powder

30ml/2 tbsp cocoa powder

115g/4oz/¾ cup dark muscovado sugar

2 eggs

150ml/¼ pint/⅔ cup soured cream

150ml/¼ pint/⅔ cup milk

60ml/4 tbsp sunflower oil

175g/6oz white chocolate

175g/6oz plain chocolate

cocoa powder, for dusting

MAKES 16

COOK'S TIP

If soured cream is not available, sour 150ml/ ¼ pint/⅔ cup single cream by stirring in 5ml/1 tsp lemon juice and letting the mixture stand until thickened.

1 Preheat the oven to 190°C/375°F/Gas 5. Place 16 paper muffin cases in muffin tins or deep patty tins. Sift the flour, baking powder and cocoa into a bowl and stir in the sugar. Make a well in the centre.

2 In a separate bowl, beat the eggs with the soured cream, milk and oil, then stir into the well in the dry ingredients. Beat well, gradually incorporating the flour mixture to make a thick and creamy batter.

3 Chop both the white and the plain chocolate into small pieces, then stir into the batter mixture.

4 Spoon the mixture into the muffin cases, filling them almost to the top. Bake for 25–30 minutes, until well risen and firm to the touch. Cool on a wire rack, then dust with cocoa powder.

CHOCOLATE MARZIPAN COOKIES

INGREDIENTS

200g/7oz/scant 1 cup unsalted butter, softened

200g/7oz/generous 1 cup light muscovado sugar

1 egg

300g/11oz/2¾ cups plain flour

60ml/4 tbsp cocoa powder

200g/7oz white almond paste

115g/4oz white chocolate, broken into squares

~ MAKES ABOUT 36 ~

Crisp little cookies for a sweet tooth, with a little almond surprise inside.

1 Preheat the oven to 190°C/375°F/Gas 5. Lightly grease two large baking sheets. Cream the butter with the sugar in a bowl until pale and fluffy. Add the egg and beat well.

2 Sift the flour and cocoa over the mixture. Stir in, first with a wooden spoon, then with clean hands, pressing the mixture together to make a fairly soft dough.

3 Roll out about half the dough on a lightly floured surface to a thickness of about 5mm/¼in. Using a 5cm/2in biscuit cutter, cut out rounds, re-rolling the dough as required until you have about 36 rounds.

4 Cut the almond paste into about 36 equal pieces. Roll into balls, flatten slightly and place one on each round of dough. Roll out the remaining dough, cut out more rounds, then place on top of the almond paste. Press the dough edges to seal.

5 Bake for 10-12 minutes, or until the cookies have risen well and are beginning to crack on the surface. Cool on the baking sheet for about 2-3 minutes, then finish cooling on a wire rack.

6 Melt the white chocolate, then either drizzle it over the biscuits to decorate, or spoon into a paper piping bag and quickly pipe a design on to the biscuits.

COOK'S TIP

If the dough is too sticky to roll, chill it for about 30 minutes, then try again.

MOCHA VIENNESE SWIRLS

INGREDIENTS

115g/4oz plain chocolate, broken into squares

200g/7oz/scant 1 cup unsalted butter, softened

50g/2oz/6 tbsp icing sugar

30ml/2 tbsp strong black coffee

200g/7oz/1¾ cups plain flour

50g/2oz/½ cup cornflour

To decorate

about 20 blanched almonds

150g/5oz plain chocolate

⁓ MAKES ABOUT 20 ⁓

1 Preheat the oven to
⁓ 190°C/375°F/Gas 5.
Lightly grease two large baking sheets. Melt the chocolate in a bowl over hot water. Cream the butter with the icing sugar in a bowl until smooth and pale. Beat in the melted chocolate, then the strong black coffee.

2 Sift the flour and cornflour
⁓ over the mixture. Fold in lightly and evenly to make a soft mixture.

3 Spoon the mixture into a
⁓ piping bag fitted with a large star nozzle and pipe about 20 swirls on the baking sheets, allowing room for spreading during baking.

4 Press an almond into the
⁓ centre of each swirl. Bake for about 15 minutes or until the biscuits are firm and just beginning to brown.

5 Leave to cool for about
⁓ 10 minutes on the baking sheets, then lift carefully on to a wire rack to cool completely.

6 When cool, melt the
⁓ chocolate and dip the base of each swirl to coat. Place on a sheet of non-stick baking paper and leave to set.

COOK'S TIP

If the mixture is too stiff to pipe, soften it with a little more black coffee.

CHUNKY DOUBLE CHOCOLATE COOKIES

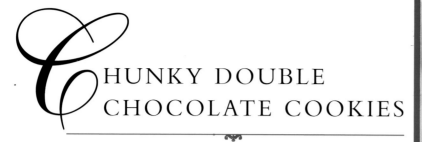

> *Keep these luscious treats under lock and key unless you're feeling generous!*

INGREDIENTS

115g/4oz/½ cup unsalted butter, softened

115g/4oz/⅔ cup light muscovado sugar

1 egg

5ml/1 tsp vanilla essence

150g/5oz/1¼ cups self-raising flour

75g/3oz/¾ cup porridge oats

115g/4oz plain chocolate, roughly chopped

115g/4oz white chocolate, roughly chopped

~ MAKES 18–20 ~

3 Place small spoonfuls of the
~ mixture in 18-20 rocky heaps on the baking sheets, leaving space for spreading.

4 Bake for 12-15 minutes or
~ until the biscuits are beginning to turn pale golden. Cool for 2-3 minutes on the baking sheets, then lift on to wire racks to cool completely.

1 Preheat the oven to
~ 190°C/375°F/Gas 5. Lightly grease two baking sheets. Cream the butter with the sugar in a bowl until pale and fluffy. Add the egg and vanilla essence and beat well.

2 Sift the flour over the
~ mixture and fold in lightly with a metal spoon, then add the oats and chopped plain and white chocolate and stir until evenly mixed.

COOK'S TIP

If you're short of time when making the cookies, substitute chocolate chips for the chopped chocolate. Chopped stem ginger would make a delicious addition as well.

CRANBERRY AND CHOCOLATE SQUARES

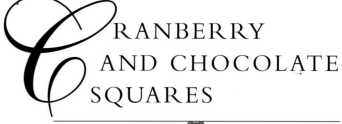

Made for each other – that's the contrasting flavours of tangy-sharp cranberries and sweet chocolate.

INGREDIENTS

150g/5oz/1¼ cups self-raising flour, plus extra for dusting

115g/4oz/½ cup unsalted butter

60ml/4 tbsp cocoa powder

215g/7½oz/1¼ cups light muscovado sugar

2 eggs, beaten

115g/4oz/1⅓ cups fresh or thawed frozen cranberries

For the topping

150ml/¼ pint/⅔ cup soured cream

75g/3oz/6 tbsp caster sugar

30ml/2 tbsp self-raising flour

50g/2oz/4 tbsp soft margarine

1 egg, beaten

2.5ml/½ tsp vanilla essence

75ml/5 tbsp coarsely grated plain chocolate for sprinkling

MAKES 12

2 Remove the melted
~ mixture from the heat and stir in the flour and eggs, beating until thoroughly mixed. Stir in the cranberries, then spread the mixture in the prepared tin.

1 Preheat the oven to
~ 180°C/350°F/Gas 4. Grease an 18 x 27cm/7 x 10½in cake tin and dust lightly with flour. Combine the butter, cocoa and sugar in a saucepan and stir over a low heat until melted and smooth.

3 Make the topping by
~ mixing all the ingredients in a bowl. Beat until smooth, then spread over the base.

4 Sprinkle with the grated
~ chocolate and bake for 40-45 minutes, or until risen and firm. Cool in the tin, then cut into 12 squares.

CHOCOLATE CINNAMON DOUGHNUTS

Serve these light and luscious treats freshly made and just warm, so that the chocolate filling melts in your mouth.

INGREDIENTS

500g/1¼lb/5 cups strong plain flour

30ml/2 tbsp cocoa powder

2.5ml/½ tsp salt

1 sachet easy-blend dried yeast

300ml/½ pint/1¼ cups hand-hot milk

40g/1½oz/3 tbsp butter, melted

1 egg, beaten

115g/4oz plain chocolate, broken into 16 pieces

sunflower oil for deep frying

For the coating

45ml/3 tbsp caster sugar

15ml/1 tbsp cocoa powder

5ml/1 tsp ground cinnamon

MAKES 16

2 Knead the dough on a lightly floured surface for about 5 minutes, until smooth and elastic. Return to the clean bowl, cover and leave in a warm place until the dough has doubled in bulk.

3 Knead the dough lightly again, then divide into 16 pieces. Shape each into a round, press a piece of plain chocolate into the centre, then fold the dough over to enclose the filling, pressing firmly to make sure the edges are sealed. Re-shape the doughnuts when sealed, if necessary.

4 Heat the oil for deep frying to 180°C/350°F or until a cube of dried bread browns in 30-45 seconds. Deep fry the doughnuts in batches. As each doughnut rises and turns golden brown, turn it over carefully to cook the other side. Drain the cooked doughnuts well on kitchen paper.

1 Sift the flour, cocoa and salt into a large bowl. Stir in the yeast. Make a well in the centre and add the milk, melted butter and egg. Stir, gradually incorporating the dry ingredients to make a soft and pliable dough.

COOK'S TIP

If you are not planning to serve the doughnuts immediately, drain them on kitchen paper, cool completely and pack in a covered container. To serve, warm the doughnuts for a few minutes in a hot oven, then toss in the coating and serve warm.

5 Mix the sugar, cocoa and cinnamon in a shallow bowl. Toss the doughnuts in the mixture to coat them evenly. Serve warm.

CHOCOLATE BUTTERSCOTCH BARS

INGREDIENTS

225g/8oz/2 cups plain flour

2.5ml/½ tsp baking powder

115g/4oz/½ cup unsalted butter

50g/2oz/⅓ cup light muscovado sugar

150g/5oz plain chocolate, melted

30ml/2 tbsp ground almonds

For the topping

175g/6oz/¾ cup unsalted butter

115g/4oz/½ cup caster sugar

30ml/2 tbsp golden syrup

175ml/6fl oz/¾ cup condensed milk

150g/5oz/1¼ cups whole
toasted hazelnuts

225g/8oz plain chocolate,
broken into squares

⌒ MAKES 24 ⌒

Unashamedly rich and sweet, these bars are perfect for chocoholics of all ages.

1 Preheat the oven to
~ 160°C/325°F/Gas 3.
Lightly grease a shallow 30 x
20cm/12 x 8in tin. Sift the
flour and baking powder into a
large bowl.

2 Rub in the butter until the
~ mixture resembles coarse
breadcrumbs, then stir in the
sugar. Work in the melted
chocolate and ground almonds
to make a light biscuit dough.

3 Press the dough evenly
~ into the prepared tin, prick
the surface with a fork and
bake for 25–30 minutes until
firm. Leave to cool in the tin.

4 Make the topping. Mix the
~ butter, sugar, golden syrup
and condensed milk in a pan.
Heat gently, stirring, until the
butter and sugar have melted.
Simmer, stirring occasionally,
until golden, then stir in the
toasted hazelnuts.

5 Pour over the cooked base.
~ Leave to set.

6 Melt the chocolate in a
~ heatproof bowl over hot
water. Spread evenly over the
butterscotch layer, then leave
to set again before cutting into
bars to serve.

COOK'S TIP

*If you prefer to cook the
bars a few days before
serving, bake the base on
its own, and add the
chocolate topping nearer
the time.*

BRIOCHES AU CHOCOLAT

Steal out of bed early and surprise the one you love with these wonderful French specialities. Light, golden and drizzled with melted chocolate, they are bound to go down well.

INGREDIENTS

250g/9oz/2¼ cups strong white flour

pinch of salt

30ml/2 tbsp caster sugar

1 sachet easy-blend dried yeast

3 eggs, beaten, plus extra beaten egg, for glazing

45ml/3 tbsp hand-hot milk

115g/4oz/½ cup unsalted butter, diced

150g/5oz plain chocolate, broken into squares

⁓ MAKES 12 ⁓

1 Sift the flour, salt and sugar into a large bowl and stir in the yeast. Make a well in the centre of the mixture and add the eggs and milk.

2 Beat well, gradually incorporating the surrounding dry ingredients to make a fairly soft dough. Turn on to a lightly floured surface and knead well until smooth and elastic, adding a little more flour if necessary.

3 Add the butter to the dough, a few pieces at a time, kneading until each addition is absorbed before adding the next. When all the butter has been incorporated and small bubbles appear in the dough, wrap it and chill for at least 1 hour, or overnight.

4 Lightly grease 12 individual brioche tins set on a baking sheet or a 12-hole brioche or patty tin. Divide the dough into 12 pieces and shape each into a smooth round. Place a chocolate square in the centre. Bring up the sides of the dough and press the edges firmly together to seal.

5 Place the brioches, join side down, in the prepared tins. Cover and leave them in a warm place for about 30 minutes or until doubled in size. Preheat the oven to 200°C/400°F/Gas 6.

6 Brush with beaten egg; bake for 12-15 minutes, until well risen and golden brown. Place on wire racks and leave until warm. Melt the remaining chocolate and drizzle it over the brioches.

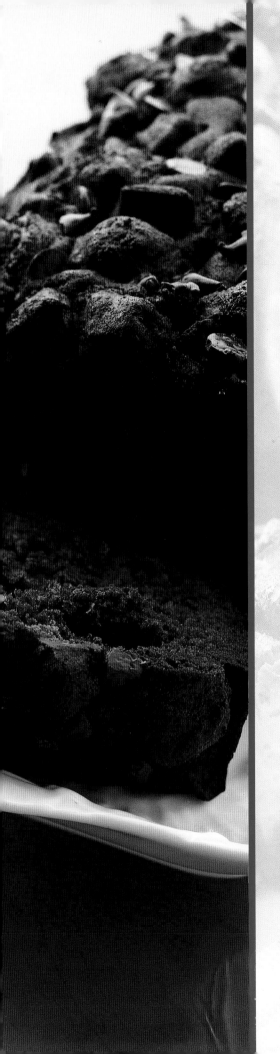

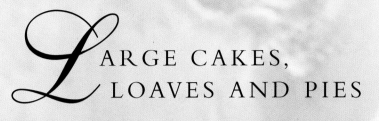

LARGE CAKES, LOAVES AND PIES

There can be few families who wouldn't leap
enthusiastically upon a simple chocolate
sponge cake, so think how they'll drool at the
sight of a deep, sticky slice of Chocolate
Pecan Pie, or Frosted Chocolate Fudge Cake.
If cheesecakes are a family favourite, try
Baked Chocolate and Raisin Cheesecake — so
simple to make and well worth it for all the
praise you'll get!

CHOCOLATE PECAN PIE

If you thought pecan pie couldn't be improved upon, just try this gorgeous chocolate one with its rich orange crust.

INGREDIENTS

200g/7oz/1¾ cups plain flour

65g/2½oz/5 tbsp caster sugar

90g/3½oz/scant ½ cup unsalted butter, softened

1 egg, beaten

finely grated rind of 1 orange

For the filling

200g/7oz/¾ cup golden syrup

45ml/3 tbsp soft light muscovado sugar

150g/5oz plain chocolate, broken into squares

50g/2oz/4 tbsp butter

3 eggs, beaten

5ml/1 tsp vanilla essence

175g/6oz/1½ cups pecan nuts

SERVES 6

1 Sift the flour into a bowl and stir in the sugar. Work in the butter evenly with the fingertips until combined.

2 Beat the egg and orange rind in a bowl, then stir into the mixture to make a firm dough. Add a little water if the mixture is too dry.

3 Roll out the pastry on a lightly floured surface and use to line a deep, 20cm/8in loose-based flan tin. Chill for 30 minutes.

4 Preheat the oven to 180°C/350°F/Gas 4. Make the filling. Mix the syrup, sugar, chocolate and butter in a small saucepan. Heat gently until melted.

5 Remove from the heat and beat in the eggs and vanilla essence. Sprinkle the pecan nuts into the pastry case and carefully pour over the chocolate mixture.

6 Place on a baking sheet and bake for 50-60 minutes or until set. Cool in the tin.

COOK'S TIP

Make individual tartlets if you prefer – use six 10cm/4in flan tins and bake at the same temperature for about 30 minutes. Walnuts or almonds can be used instead of pecan nuts.

FROSTED CHOCOLATE FUDGE CAKE

> *Rich and dreamy, with an irresistible chocolate fudgy frosting, this cake couldn't be easier to make, or more wonderful to eat!*

INGREDIENTS

115g/4oz plain chocolate, broken into squares

175g/6oz/¾ cup unsalted butter or margarine, softened

200g/7oz/generous 1 cup light muscovado sugar

5ml/1 tsp vanilla essence

3 eggs, beaten

150ml/¼ pint/⅔ cup Greek-style yogurt

150g/5oz/1¼ cups self-raising flour

icing sugar and chocolate curls, to decorate

For the frosting

115g/4oz plain dark chocolate, broken into squares

50g/2oz/4 tbsp unsalted butter

350g/12oz/3 cups icing sugar

90ml/6 tbsp Greek-style yogurt

≈ SERVES 6–8 ≈

COOK'S TIP

If the frosting begins to set too quickly, heat it gently to soften, and beat in a little extra yogurt if necessary.

1 Preheat the oven to 190°C/375°F/Gas 5. Grease two 20cm/8in round sandwich cake tins and line the base of each with non-stick baking paper. Melt the chocolate in a heatproof bowl over hot water.

2 In a mixing bowl, cream the butter or margarine with the sugar until light and fluffy. Beat in the vanilla essence, then gradually add the beaten eggs, beating well after each addition.

3 Stir in the melted plain chocolate and yogurt evenly. Fold in the flour with a metal spoon.

4 Divide the mixture between the prepared tins. Bake for 25–30 minutes or until the cakes are firm to the touch. Turn out and cool on a wire rack.

5 Make the frosting. Melt the chocolate and butter in a saucepan over a low heat. Remove from the heat and stir in the icing sugar and yogurt. Mix with a rubber spatula until smooth, then beat until the frosting begins to cool and thicken slightly. Use about a third of the mixture to sandwich the cakes together.

6 Working quickly, spread the remainder over the top and sides. Sprinkle with icing sugar and decorate with chocolate curls.

CHOCOLATE GINGER CRUNCH CAKE

INGREDIENTS

150g/5oz plain chocolate,
broken into squares

50g/2oz/4 tbsp unsalted butter

115g/4oz ginger nut biscuits

4 pieces preserved stem ginger

30ml/2 tbsp stem ginger syrup

45ml/3 tbsp desiccated coconut

To decorate

25g/1oz milk chocolate

pieces of crystallized ginger

~ SERVES 6 ~

Ginger adds a flicker of fire to this delectable uncooked cake. Keep one in the fridge for midnight feasts and other late-night treats.

1 Grease a 15cm/6in flan ring; place it on a sheet of non-stick baking paper. Melt the plain chocolate with the butter in a heatproof bowl over barely simmering water. Remove from the heat.

3 Chop the stem ginger fairly finely and mix with the crushed biscuits.

5 Tip the mixture into the prepared flan ring and press down firmly and evenly. Chill in the fridge until set.

6 Remove the flan ring and slide the cake on to a plate. Melt the milk chocolate, drizzle it over the top and decorate with the pieces of crystallized ginger.

2 Crush the biscuits into small pieces (see Cook's Tip). Tip them into a bowl.

4 Stir the biscuit mixture, ginger syrup and coconut into the melted chocolate and butter, mixing well until evenly combined.

COOK'S TIP

Do not crumb the biscuits, as you need some crunchy pieces for texture. Put them in a stout plastic bag and crush them with a rolling pin, or chop them in a food processor, using the pulse setting for greater control.

BAKED CHOCOLATE AND RAISIN CHEESECAKE

INGREDIENTS

75g/3oz/¾ cup plain flour

45ml/3 tbsp cocoa powder

75g/3oz/½ cup semolina

50g/2oz/¼ cup caster sugar

115g/4oz/½ cup unsalted
butter, softened

For the filling

225g/8oz/1 cup cream cheese

120ml/4fl oz/½ cup natural yogurt

2 eggs, beaten

75g/3oz/6 tbsp caster sugar

finely grated rind of 1 lemon

75g/3oz/½ cup raisins

45ml/3 tbsp plain chocolate chips

For the topping

75g/3oz plain chocolate,
broken into squares

30ml/2 tbsp golden syrup

40g/1½oz/3 tbsp butter

☞ SERVES 8–10 ☜

If you just can't get enough chocolate, this delectable cheesecake will be your idea of heaven. Its crisp chocolate shortbread base is covered with a creamy chocolate chip filling, topped off with a sticky chocolate glaze.

1 Preheat the oven to
~ 150°C/300°F/Gas 2. Sift
the flour and cocoa into a
mixing bowl and stir in the
semolina and sugar. Using your
fingertips, work the butter into
the flour mixture until it makes
a firm dough.

2 Press the dough into the
~ base of a 22cm/8½ in
springform tin. Prick all over
with a fork and bake in the
oven for 15 minutes. Remove
the tin but leave the oven on.

3 Make the filling. In a large
~ bowl, beat the cream
cheese with the yogurt, eggs
and sugar until evenly mixed.
Stir in the lemon rind, raisins
and chocolate chips.

COOK'S TIP

*For a slightly quicker
version, omit the topping
and simply drizzle
melted chocolate over the
cheesecake to finish.*

4 Smooth the cream cheese
~ mixture over the chocolate
shortbread base and bake for a
further 35–45 minutes, or until
the filling is pale gold and just
set. Cool in the tin.

5 To make the topping,
~ combine the chocolate,
syrup and butter in a heatproof
bowl. Set over a saucepan of
simmering water and heat
gently, stirring occasionally,
until melted. Pour over the
cheesecake and leave until set.

CHOCOLATE CHIP MARZIPAN LOAF

INGREDIENTS

115g/4oz/½ cup unsalted butter, softened

150g/5oz/scant 1 cup light muscovado sugar

2 eggs

45ml/3 tbsp cocoa powder

150g/5oz/1¼ cups self-raising flour

130g/4½oz marzipan

60ml/4 tbsp plain chocolate chips

MAKES 1 LOAF

Sometimes plain wrappers disguise the most marvellous surprises. Inside this ordinary-looking loaf are creamy chunks of marzipan and chips of chocolate.

1 Preheat the oven to 180°C/350°F/Gas 4. Grease a 900g/2lb loaf tin and line the base with non-stick baking paper. Cream the butter and sugar in a mixing bowl until light and fluffy.

2 Add the eggs to the creamed mixture one at a time, beating well after each addition to combine.

3 Sift the cocoa and flour over the mixture and fold in evenly.

4 Chop the marzipan into small pieces with a sharp knife. Tip into a bowl and mix with the chocolate chips. Set aside about 60ml/4 tbsp and fold the rest evenly into the cake mixture.

5 Scrape the mixture into the prepared tin, level the top and scatter with the reserved marzipan and chocolate chips.

6 Bake for 45–50 minutes or until the loaf is risen and firm. Cool for a few minutes in the tin, then turn out on to a wire rack to cool completely.

COOK'S TIP

This cake is ideal for freezing, either whole or in handy slices separated by sheets of freezer film. Wrap it in foil and freeze for up to 3 months.

STICKY CHOCOLATE, MAPLE AND WALNUT SWIRLS

INGREDIENTS

450g/1lb/4 cups strong white flour

2.5ml/½ tsp ground cinnamon

50g/2oz/4 tbsp unsalted butter

50g/2oz/¼ cup caster sugar

1 sachet easy-blend dried yeast

1 egg yolk

120ml/4fl oz/½ cup water

60ml/4 tbsp milk

45ml/3 tbsp maple syrup, to finish

For the filling

40g/1½oz/3 tbsp unsalted butter, melted

50g/2oz/⅓ cup light muscovado sugar

175g/6oz/1 cup plain chocolate chips

75g/3oz/¾ cup chopped walnuts

SERVES 12

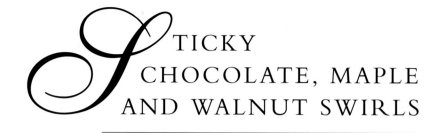

This rich yeasted cake breaks into separate sticky chocolate swirls, each soaked in maple syrup.

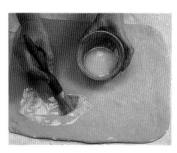

1 Grease a deep 23cm/9in
~ springform cake tin. Sift the flour and cinnamon into a bowl, then rub in the butter until the mixture resembles coarse breadcrumbs.

2 Stir in the sugar and yeast.
~ In a jug or bowl, beat the egg yolk with the water and milk, then stir into the dry ingredients to make a soft dough (see Cook's Tip).

3 Knead the dough on a
~ lightly floured surface until smooth, then roll out to a rectangle measuring about 40 x 30cm/16 x 12in.

4 For the filling, brush the
~ dough with the melted butter and sprinkle with the sugar, chocolate chips and nuts.

5 Roll up the dough from
~ one long side like a Swiss roll, then cut into 12 thick even-size slices.

6 Pack the slices closely
~ together in the prepared tin, with the cut sides facing upwards. Cover and leave in a warm place for about 1½ hours, until well risen and springy to the touch. Meanwhile, preheat the oven to 220°C/425°F/Gas 7.

7 Bake the swirls for about
~ 30-35 minutes until well risen, golden brown and firm. Remove from the tin and cool on a wire rack. To finish, spoon or brush the maple syrup over the cake. Pull the pieces apart to serve.

COOK'S TIP

The amount of liquid added to the dry ingredients may have to be adjusted slightly as some flours absorb more liquid than others. The dough should be soft but not sticky.

BITTER MARMALADE CHOCOLATE LOAF

INGREDIENTS

115g/4oz plain chocolate, broken into squares

3 eggs

200g/7oz/scant 1 cup caster sugar

175ml/6fl oz/¾ cup soured cream

200g/7oz/1¾ cups self-raising flour

For the filling and glaze

175g/6oz/⅔ cup bitter orange marmalade

115g/4oz plain chocolate, broken into squares

60ml/4 tbsp soured cream

shredded orange rind, to decorate

~ SERVES 8 ~

Don't be alarmed at the amount of cream in this recipe – it's naughty but necessary, and replaces butter to make a moist dark cake, topped with a bitter-sweet sticky marmalade topping.

1 Preheat the oven to 180°C/350°F/Gas 4. Grease a 900g/2lb loaf tin lightly, then line it with non-stick baking paper. Melt the chocolate in a heatproof bowl over hot water.

2 Combine the eggs and sugar in a separate bowl. Using a hand-held electric mixer, whisk the mixture until it is thick and creamy, then stir in the soured cream and chocolate. Fold in the self-raising flour evenly.

3 Scrape the mixture into the prepared tin and bake for about 1 hour or until well risen and firm to the touch. Cool for a few minutes in the tin, then turn out on to a wire rack and leave to cool completely.

4 Make the filling. Spoon two-thirds of the marmalade into a small saucepan and melt over a gentle heat. Melt the chocolate and stir it into the marmalade with the soured cream.

5 Slice the cake across into three layers and sandwich back together with about half the marmalade filling. Spread the rest over the top of the cake and leave to set. Spoon the remaining marmalade over the cake and scatter with shredded orange rind, to decorate.

COOK'S TIP

If you don't particularly like marmalade, use apricot jam instead.

CHOCOLATE AND CHERRY POLENTA CAKE

Perfect for packing to take on a romantic picnic, this chocolate cherry cake is dense and delicious. Polenta and almonds add an unusual nutty texture.

INGREDIENTS

50g/2oz/⅓ cup quick-cook polenta

200g/7oz plain chocolate, broken into squares

5 eggs, separated

175g/6oz/¾ cup caster sugar

115g/4oz/1 cup ground almonds

60ml/4 tbsp plain flour

finely grated rind of 1 orange

115g/4oz/½ cup glacé cherries, halved

icing sugar, for dusting

~ SERVES 8 ~

1 Place the polenta in a
~ heatproof bowl and pour over just enough boiling water to cover; about 120ml/4fl oz/ ½ cup. Stir well, then cover the bowl and leave to stand for about 30 minutes, until the polenta has absorbed all the excess moisture.

2 Preheat the oven to
~ 190°C/375°F/Gas 5.
Grease a deep 22cm/8½in round cake tin and line the base with non-stick baking paper. Melt the chocolate in a heatproof bowl over hot water.

3 Whisk the egg yolks with
~ the sugar in a bowl until thick and pale. Beat in the chocolate, then fold in the polenta, ground almonds, flour and orange rind.

COOK'S TIP

*It is important to add only just enough water to cover the polenta, as too much moisture in the mixture will cause the cherries to sink.
If necessary, drain off excess moisture.*

4 Whisk the egg whites in a
~ clean, grease-free bowl until stiff. Stir about 15ml/ 1 tbsp of the whites into the chocolate mixture to lighten it, then fold in the rest. Finally, fold in the cherries.

5 Scrape the mixture into the
~ prepared tin and bake for 45-55 minutes or until well risen and firm to the touch. Turn out and cool on a wire rack, then dust with icing sugar to serve.

MARBLED SWISS ROLL

WITH CHOCOLATE AND WALNUT BUTTERCREAM

INGREDIENTS

90g/3½oz/scant 1 cup plain flour

15ml/1 tbsp cocoa powder

25g/1oz plain chocolate, grated

25g/1oz white chocolate, grated

3 eggs

115g/4oz/½ cup caster sugar

30ml/2 tbsp boiling water

For the filling

1 quantity Chocolate Buttercream

45ml/3 tbsp chopped walnuts

⁓ SERVES 6 – 8 ⁓

Simply sensational – that's the combination of light chocolate sponge and walnut chocolate buttercream.

1 Preheat the oven to 200°C/400°F/Gas 6. Grease a 30 x 20cm/12 x 8in Swiss roll tin and line with non-stick baking paper. Sift half the flour with the cocoa into bowl. Stir in the grated plain chocolate. Sift the remaining flour into another bowl; stir in the grated white chocolate.

2 Whisk the eggs and sugar in a heatproof bowl; set over a saucepan of hot water until it holds its shape when the whisk is lifted.

3 Remove the bowl from the heat and tip half the mixture into a separate bowl. Fold the white chocolate mixture into one portion, then fold the plain chocolate mixture into the other. Stir 15ml/1 tbsp boiling water into each half to soften the mixtures.

4 Place alternate spoonfuls of mixture in the prepared tin and swirl lightly together for a marbled effect. Bake for about 12-15 minutes, or until firm. Turn out on to a sheet of non-stick baking paper.

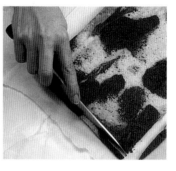

5 Trim the edges to neaten and cover with a damp, clean dish towel. Cool.

6 For the filling, mix the buttercream and walnuts in a bowl. Uncover the sponge, lift off the lining paper and spread the surface with the buttercream. Roll up carefully from a long side and place on a serving plate. Decorate with plain and white chocolate curls, if wished.

COOK'S TIP

Use a skewer to swirl the chocolate and plain mixtures together. Make sure that the mixture fills the corners of the tin.

SIMPLE SCHOLOLATE CAKE

An easy, everyday chocolate cake which can be simply filled with buttercream, or pepped up with a rich chocolate ganache for a special occasion.

INGREDIENTS

115g/4oz plain chocolate, broken into squares

45ml/3 tbsp milk

150g/5oz/⅔ cup unsalted butter or margarine, softened

150g/5oz/scant 1 cup light muscovado sugar

3 eggs

200g/7oz/1¾ cups self-raising flour

15ml/1 tbsp cocoa powder

1 quantity Chocolate Buttercream, for the filling

icing sugar and cocoa powder, for dusting

SERVES 6–8

1 Preheat the oven to 180°C/350°F/Gas 4. Grease two 18cm/7in round sandwich cake tins and line the base of each with non-stick baking paper. Melt the chocolate with the milk in a heatproof bowl set over a pan of simmering water.

2 Cream the butter or margarine with the sugar in a mixing bowl until pale and fluffy. Add the eggs one at a time, beating well after each addition. Stir in the chocolate mixture until well combined.

COOK'S TIP

For a richer finish, make a double quantity of buttercream and spread or pipe over the top of the cake as well as using for the filling.

3 Sift the flour and cocoa over the mixture and fold in with a metal spoon until evenly mixed. Scrape into the prepared tins, smooth level and bake for 35–40 minutes or until well risen and firm. Turn out on wire racks to cool.

4 Sandwich the cake layers together with the buttercream. Dust with a mixture of icing sugar and cocoa just before serving.

SPECIAL OCCASION CAKES

Any special celebration is a good excuse for indulgence and nothing could be more indulgent than a luxuriously rich chocolate gâteau or a lavish Sachertorte, or try out your skills on a more unusual, impressive Rich Chocolate Leaf Gâteau. Alternatively, you could disregard everyone's diet and go totally overboard with the richest chocolate cake ever – Death by Chocolate!

SACHERTORTE

Rich and dark, with a wonderful flavour, this glorious gâteau was created in Vienna in 1832 by Franz Sacher, a chef in the royal household.

INGREDIENTS

225g/8oz plain dark chocolate, broken into squares

150g/5oz/⅔ cup unsalted butter, softened

115g/4oz/½ cup caster sugar

8 eggs, separated

115g/4oz/1 cup plain flour

For the glaze

225g/8oz/1 cup apricot jam

15ml/1 tbsp lemon juice

For the icing

225g/8oz plain dark chocolate, broken into squares

200g/7oz/scant 1 cup caster sugar

15ml/1 tbsp golden syrup

250ml/8fl oz/1 cup double cream

5ml/1 tsp vanilla essence

plain chocolate curls, to decorate

~ SERVES 10–12 ~

2 Cream the butter with the sugar in a mixing bowl until pale and fluffy, then add the egg yolks, one at a time, beating after each addition. Beat in the melted chocolate, then sift the flour over the mixture and fold it in evenly.

3 Whisk the egg whites in a clean, grease-free bowl until stiff, then stir about a quarter of the whites into the chocolate mixture to lighten it. Fold in the remaining whites.

4 Tip the mixture into the prepared cake tin and smooth level. Bake for about 50-55 minutes, or until firm. Turn out carefully on to a wire rack to cool.

5 Make the glaze. Heat the apricot jam with the lemon juice in a small saucepan until melted, then strain through a sieve into a bowl. Once the cake is cold, slice in half across the middle to make two even-size layers.

7 Make the icing. Mix the chocolate, sugar, golden syrup, cream and vanilla essence in a heavy saucepan. Heat gently, stirring constantly, until the mixture is thick and smooth. Simmer gently for 3-4 minutes, without stirring, until the mixture registers 95°C/200°F on a sugar thermometer. Pour the icing quickly over the cake, spreading to cover the top and sides completely. Leave to set, decorate with chocolate curls, then serve with whipped cream if wished.

1 Preheat the oven to 180°C/350°F/Gas 4. Grease a 23cm/9in round springform cake tin and line with non-stick baking paper. Melt the chocolate in a heatproof bowl over hot water, then remove from the heat.

6 Brush the top and sides of each layer with the apricot glaze, then sandwich them together. Place on a wire rack.

COOK'S TIP

Use the finest dark chocolate you can afford to make this gâteau – the expense will be amply justified.

CHOCOLATE ROULADE

WITH COCONUT WHISKY CREAM

INGREDIENTS

150g/5oz/¾ cup caster sugar

5 eggs, separated

50g/2oz/½ cup cocoa powder

For the filling

300ml/½ pint/1¼ cups double cream

45ml/3 tbsp whisky

50g/2oz piece solid
creamed coconut

30ml/2 tbsp caster sugar

For the topping

coarsely grated curls of fresh coconut

chocolate curls

~ SERVES 8 ~

A ravishing roulade topped with curls of fresh coconut, perfect for that special anniversary.

1 Preheat the oven to
~ 180°C/350°C/Gas 4.
Grease a 32 x 23cm/13 x 9in
Swiss roll tin. Dust a large
sheet of greaseproof paper with
30ml/2 tsbp of the caster sugar.

2 Place the egg yolks in a
~ heatproof bowl. Add the
remaining caster sugar and
whisk with a hand-held
electric mixer until the
mixture is thick enough to
leave a trail. Sift the cocoa
over, then fold in carefully and
evenly with a metal spoon.

3 Whisk the egg whites in a
~ clean, grease-free bowl
until they form soft peaks.
Fold about 15ml/1 tbsp of the
whites into the chocolate
mixture to lighten it, then fold
in the rest evenly.

4 Scrape the mixture into the
~ prepared tin, taking it right
into the corners. Smooth the
surface with a palette knife,
then bake for 20-25 minutes or
until well risen and springy to
the touch.

5 Turn the cooked roulade
~ out on to the sugar-dusted
greaseproof paper and carefully
peel off the lining paper. Cover
with a damp, clean dish towel
and leave to cool.

6 Make the filling. Whisk the
~ cream with the whisky in a
bowl until the mixture just
holds its shape, then finely
grate the creamed coconut and
stir it in with the sugar.

7 Uncover the sponge and
~ spread about three-quarters
of the cream mixture to the
edges. Roll up carefully from a
long side. Transfer to a plate,
pipe or spoon the remaining
cream mixture on top, then
make the coconut curls and
place on top with the
chocolate curls.

WHITE CHOCOLATE CAPPUCCINO GATEAU

Luscious, lavish and laced with liqueur, this is strictly for adults only!

INGREDIENTS

4 eggs

115g/4oz/½ cup caster sugar

15ml/1 tbsp strong black coffee

2.5ml/½ tsp vanilla essence

115g/4oz/1 cup plain flour

75g/3oz white chocolate,
coarsely grated

For the filling

120ml/4fl oz/½ cup double cream

15ml/1 tbsp coffee liqueur

For the frosting and topping

15ml/1 tbsp coffee liqueur

1 quantity White Chocolate Frosting

white chocolate curls

cocoa powder or powdered cinnamon,
for dusting

SERVES 8

COOK'S TIP

If you don't have any coffee liqueur, use brandy or dark rum instead. For an alcohol-free version, substitute strong black coffee.

1 Preheat the oven to 180°C/350°F/Gas 4. Grease two 19cm/7½in round sandwich cake tins and line the base of each with non-stick baking paper.

2 Combine the eggs, caster sugar, coffee and vanilla essence in a large heatproof bowl. Place over a saucepan of hot water and whisk until the mixture is pale and thick enough to hold its shape when the whisk is lifted.

3 Sift half the flour over the mixture; fold in gently and evenly. Carefully fold in the remaining flour with the grated white chocolate.

4 Divide the mixture between the prepared tins and smooth level. Bake for 20-25 minutes, until firm and golden brown, then turn out on wire racks and leave to cool completely.

5 Make the filling. Whip the cream with the coffee liqueur in a bowl until it holds its shape. Spread over one of the cakes, then place the second layer on top.

6 Stir the coffee liqueur into the frosting. Spread over the top and sides of the cake, swirling with a palette knife. Top with curls of white chocolate and dust with cocoa or cinnamon.

CHOCOLATE REDCURRANT TORTE

3 Spoon the mixture into the prepared tin and smooth the surface level. Bake for 40–50 minutes or until well risen and firm. Turn out on to a wire rack and leave to cool completely.

Redcurrants are perfect partners for chocolate in this glossy gâteau, as their slightly sharp-sweet flavour balances the rich chocolate beautifully.

INGREDIENTS

115g/4oz/½ cup unsalted
butter, softened

115g/4oz/⅔ cup dark muscovado sugar

2 eggs

150ml/¼ pint/⅔ cup soured cream

150g/5oz/1¼ cups self-raising flour

5ml/1 tsp baking powder

45ml/3 tbsp cocoa powder

75g/3oz/¾ cup stemmed redcurrants,
plus 115g/4oz/1 cup redcurrant
sprigs, to decorate

For the icing

150g/5oz plain chocolate,
broken into squares

45ml/3 tbsp redcurrant jelly

30ml/2 tbsp dark rum

120ml/4fl oz/½ cup double cream

🍃 SERVES 8–10 🍃

COOK'S TIP

If redcurrants are not available, use other small soft fruits such as raspberries or blackcurrants instead.

1 Preheat the oven to 180°C/350°F/Gas 4. Grease a 1.2 litre/2 pint/5 cup ring tin and dust lightly with flour. Cream the butter with the sugar in a mixing bowl until pale and fluffy. Beat in the eggs and soured cream until thoroughly mixed.

2 Sift the flour, baking powder and cocoa over the mixture, then fold in lightly and evenly. Fold in the stemmed redcurrants.

4 Make the icing. Mix the chocolate, redcurrant jelly and rum in a heatproof bowl. Set the bowl over simmering water and heat gently, stirring occasionally, until melted. Remove from the heat and stir in the cream.

5 Transfer the cooked cake to a serving plate. Spoon the icing evenly over the cake, allowing it to drizzle down the sides. Decorate with redcurrant sprigs just before serving.

CHOCOLATE ALMOND MOUSSE CAKE

Surrender to a taste sensation with this superb combination of chocolate and almonds.

INGREDIENTS

50g/2oz plain dark chocolate, broken into squares

200g/7oz marzipan, grated or chopped

200ml/7fl oz/scant 1 cup milk

115g/4oz/1 cup self-raising flour

2 eggs, separated

75g/3oz/½ cup light muscovado sugar

For the mousse filling

115g/4oz plain chocolate, broken into squares

50g/2oz/4 tbsp unsalted butter

2 eggs, separated

30ml/2 tbsp Amaretto di Saronno liqueur

For the topping

1 quantity Chocolate Ganache

toasted flaked almonds, to decorate

 SERVES 8

1 Preheat the oven to 190°C/375°F/Gas 5. Grease a deep 17cm/6½in square cake tin and line with non-stick baking paper. Combine the chocolate, marzipan and milk in a saucepan and heat gently without boiling, stirring until melted and smooth.

2 Sift the flour into a bowl and add the chocolate mixture and egg yolks, beating until evenly mixed.

3 Whisk the egg whites in a clean, grease-free bowl until stiff enough to hold firm peaks. Whisk in the sugar gradually. Stir about 15ml/1 tbsp of the whites into the chocolate mixture to lighten it, then fold in the rest.

4 Spoon the mixture into the tin, spreading it evenly. Bake for 45-50 minutes, until well risen, firm and springy to the touch. Leave to cool on a wire rack.

5 Make the mousse filling. Melt the chocolate with the butter in a heatproof bowl over barely simmering water, then remove from the heat and beat in the egg yolks and Amaretto. Whisk the egg whites in a clean, grease-free bowl until stiff, then fold into the chocolate mixture.

6 Slice the cold cake in half across the middle to make two even layers. Return one half to the clean cake tin and pour over the chocolate mousse. Top with the second layer of cake and press down lightly. Chill until set.

7 Turn the cake out on to a serving plate. Spread the chocolate ganache over the top and sides, then press toasted, flaked almonds over the sides. Serve chilled.

COOK'S TIP

It is important that the chocolate mixture is hot when you beat in the yolks, so that they cook slightly.

DEATH BY CHOCOLATE

INGREDIENTS

225g/8oz plain dark chocolate, broken into squares

115g/4oz/½ cup unsalted butter

150ml/¼ pint/⅔ cup milk

225g/8oz/1¼ cups light muscovado sugar

10ml/2 tsp vanilla essence

2 eggs, separated

150ml/¼ pint/⅔ cup soured cream

225g/8oz/2 cups self-raising flour

5ml/1 tsp baking powder

For the filling and topping

60ml/4 tbsp seedless raspberry jam

60ml/4 tbsp brandy

400g/14oz plain dark chocolate, broken into squares

200g/7oz/scant 1 cup unsalted butter

1 quantity Chocolate Ganache

plain and white chocolate curls, to decorate

☞ SERVES 16–20 ☜

One of the richest chocolate cakes ever, this should be served in thin slices. True chocoholics can always come back for more!

1 Preheat the oven to 180°C/350°F/Gas 4. Grease and base-line a deep 23cm/9in springform cake tin. Place the chocolate, butter and milk in a saucepan. Stir over a low heat until smooth. Remove from the heat, beat in the sugar and vanilla, then leave to cool slightly.

2 Beat the egg yolks and cream in a bowl, then beat into the chocolate mixture. Sift the flour and baking powder over the surface and fold in.

3 Whisk the egg whites in a grease-free bowl until stiff; fold into the mixture.

4 Scrape into the prepared tin and bake for about 45–55 minutes, or until firm to the touch. Cool in the tin for 15 minutes, then invert on to a wire rack to cool.

5 Slice the cold cake across the middle to make three even layers. Make the filling. In a small saucepan, warm the jam with 15ml/1 tbsp of the brandy, then brush over two of the layers; leave to set. Place the remaining brandy in a saucepan with the chocolate and butter. Heat gently, stirring, until smooth. Cool until beginning to thicken.

6 Spread the bottom layer of the cake with half the chocolate filling, taking care not to disturb the jam. Top with a second layer, jam side up, and spread with the remaining filling. Top with the final layer and press lightly.

7 Leave to set, then spread the top and sides of the cake with the chocolate ganache. Decorate with chocolate curls and, if liked, chocolate-dipped physalis (Cape gooseberries).

COOK'S TIP

You may find it easier to reassemble the cake in the clean cake tin. Turn it out on to a plate when set, then cover in chocolate ganache.

BLACK FOREST GATEAU

This luscious light chocolate sponge, moistened with Kirsch and layered with cherries and cream, is still one of the most popular chocolate gâteaux.

INGREDIENTS

6 eggs

200g/7oz/scant 1 cup caster sugar

5ml/1 tsp vanilla essence

50g/2oz/½ cup plain flour

50g/2oz/½ cup cocoa powder

115g/4oz/½ cup unsalted butter, melted

For the filling and topping

60ml/4 tbsp Kirsch

600ml/1 pint/2½ cups double or whipping cream

30ml/2 tbsp icing sugar

2.5ml/½ tsp vanilla essence

675g/1½lb jar stoned morello cherries, drained

To decorate

icing sugar, for dusting

grated chocolate

chocolate curls

fresh or drained canned morello cherries

SERVES 8–10

1 Preheat the oven to 180°C/350°F/Gas 4. Grease three 19cm/7½in sandwich cake tins and line the base of each with non-stick baking paper. Whisk the eggs with the sugar and vanilla essence in a bowl until pale and very thick - the mixture should hold a firm trail when the whisk is lifted.

2 Sift the flour and cocoa over the mixture and fold in lightly and evenly. Stir in the melted butter.

3 Divide the mixture among the prepared cake tins, smoothing them level. Bake for 15-18 minutes, until risen and springy to the touch. Leave to cool in the tins for about 5 minutes, then turn out on to wire racks and leave to cool completely.

4 Prick each layer all over with a skewer or fork, then sprinkle with Kirsch. Whip the cream in a bowl until it starts to thicken, then beat in the icing sugar and vanilla essence until the mixture begins to hold its shape.

5 To assemble, spread one cake layer with a thick layer of flavoured cream and top with a quarter of the cherries. Spread a second cake layer with cream and cherries, then place it on top of the first layer. Top with the final layer.

6 Spread the remaining cream all over the cake. Dust a plate with icing sugar; position the cake. Press grated chocolate over the sides and decorate with the chocolate curls and cherries.

Meringue Pyramid with Chocolate Mascarpone

Roses spell romance for this impressive cake. It makes the perfect centrepiece for a celebration buffet table, and most of the preparation can be done in advance.

INGREDIENTS

4 egg whites

pinch of salt

175g/6oz/¾ cup caster sugar

5ml/1 tsp ground cinnamon

75g/3oz plain dark chocolate, grated

icing sugar and rose petals, to decorate

For the filling

115g/4oz plain chocolate, broken into squares

5ml/1 tsp vanilla essence or rosewater

115g/4oz/½ cup mascarpone cheese

SERVES ABOUT 10

1 Preheat the oven to
~ 150°C/300°F/Gas 2. Line two large baking sheets with non-stick baking paper. Whisk the egg whites with the salt in a clean, grease-free bowl until they form stiff peaks.

2 Gradually whisk in half the
~ sugar, then add the rest and whisk until the meringue is very stiff and glossy. Add the cinnamon and chocolate and whisk lightly to mix.

3 Draw a 20cm/8in circle on
~ the lining paper on one of the baking sheets, replace it upside down, and spread the marked circle evenly with about half the meringue. Spoon the remaining meringue in 28–30 small neat heaps on both baking sheets. Bake for 1–1½ hours, or until crisp.

4 Make the filling. Melt the
~ chocolate in a heatproof bowl over hot water. Cool slightly, then add the vanilla essence or rosewater and cheese. Cool the mixture until it holds its shape.

5 Spoon the chocolate
~ mixture into a large piping bag and sandwich the meringues together in pairs, reserving a small amount of filling for the pyramid.

6 Arrange the filled
~ meringues on a serving platter, piling them up in a pyramid and keeping them in position with a few well-placed dabs of the reserved filling. Dust the pyramid with icing sugar, sprinkle with the rose petals and serve.

COOK'S TIP

The meringues can be made up to a week in advance and stored in an airtight container in a cool, dry place.

RICH CHOCOLATE LEAF GATEAU

INGREDIENTS

150ml/¼ pint/⅔ cup milk

75g/3oz plain dark chocolate, broken into squares

175g/6oz/¾ cup unsalted butter, softened

250g/9oz/1½ cups light muscovado sugar

3 eggs

250g/9oz/2¼ cups plain flour

10ml/2 tsp baking powder

75ml/5 tbsp single cream

For the filling and topping

60ml/4 tbsp raspberry conserve

1 quantity Chocolate Ganache

dark and white chocolate leaves

⟫ SERVES 12–14 ⟪

Thick, creamy chocolate ganache and chocolate leaves decorate this mouth-watering gâteau.

1 Preheat the oven to
~ 190°C/375°F/Gas 5.
Grease two 22cm/8½in
sandwich cake tins and line the
base of each with non-stick
baking paper. Stir the milk and
chocolate over a low heat until
the chocolate has melted.
Allow to cool slightly.

3 Sift the flour and baking
~ powder over the mixture
and fold in. Stir in the melted
chocolate mixture with the
cream, mixing until smooth.

4 Divide between the
~ prepared tins and level the
tops. Bake for 30–35 minutes
or until the cakes are well risen
and firm to the touch. Cool in
the tins for a few minutes, then
turn out on to wire racks.

5 Sandwich the cake layers
~ together with all the
raspberry conserve.

6 Spread the chocolate
~ ganache over the top and
sides of the cake. Swirl the
ganache with a knife. Place the
cake on a serving plate, then
decorate with the dark and
white chocolate leaves.

COOK'S TIP

Make a mixture of dark, milk and white chocolate leaves, or marble the mixtures for a variegated effect. Prepare the chocolate leaves in advance to save time, and store them in a covered container in a cool, dry place.

2 Cream the butter with the
~ sugar in a mixing bowl
until pale and fluffy. Beat in
the eggs one at a time, beating
well after each addition.

CARIBBEAN CHOCOLATE RING WITH RUM SYRUP

INGREDIENTS

115g/4oz/½ cup unsalted butter

115g/4oz/¾ cup light muscovado sugar

2 eggs, beaten

2 ripe bananas, mashed

30ml/2 tbsp desiccated coconut

30ml/2 tbsp soured cream

115g/4oz/1 cup self-raising flour

2.5ml/½ tsp bicarbonate of soda

45ml/3 tbsp cocoa

For the syrup

115g/4oz/½ cup caster sugar

60ml/4 tbsp water

30ml/2 tbsp dark rum

50g/2oz plain dark chocolate, chopped

To decorate

mixture of tropical fruits, such as mango, pawpaw, starfruit and cape gooseberries

chocolate shapes or curls

SERVES 8–10

Lavish and colourful, this exotic chocolate gâteau can be made in advance, then, just before serving, add the syrup and fruit.

1 Preheat the oven to
~ 180°C/350°F/Gas 4.
Grease a 1.5 litre/2½ pint/
6¼ cup ring tin.

2 Cream together the butter
~ and sugar until light and
fluffy. Beat in the eggs
gradually, beating well, then
mix in the bananas, coconut
and cream.

3 Sift the flour, cocoa and
~ bicarbonate of soda over
the mixture and fold in
thoroughly and evenly.

4 Tip into the prepared tin
~ and spread evenly. Bake for
45–50 minutes, until firm to
the touch. Cool for about
10 minutes in the tin, then
turn out to finish cooling on a
wire rack.

5 For the syrup, place the
~ sugar and water in a pan
and heat gently until dissolved.
Bring to the boil and boil
rapidly for 2 minutes. Remove
from the heat.

6 Add the rum and chocolate
~ and stir until melted and
smooth, then spoon evenly
over the cake.

7 Decorate the ring with
~ tropical fruits and chocolate
shapes or curls.

COOK'S TIP

For a really good chocolate flavour, use a good quality plain dark chocolate for the syrup.

CHOCOLATE BRANDY SNAP GATEAU

INGREDIENTS

225g/8oz plain dark chocolate, broken into squares

225g/8oz/1 cup unsalted butter, softened

200g/7oz/generous 1 cup dark muscovado sugar

6 eggs, separated

5ml/1 tsp vanilla essence

150g/5oz/1¼ cups ground hazelnuts

60ml/4 tbsp fresh white breadcrumbs

finely grated rind of 1 large orange

1 quantity Chocolate Ganache, for filling and frosting

icing sugar, for dusting

For the Brandy Snaps

50g/2oz/4 tbsp unsalted butter

50g/2oz/¼ cup caster sugar

75g/3oz/⅓ cup golden syrup

50g/2oz/½ cup plain flour

5ml/1 tsp brandy

↝ SERVES 8 ↜

1 Preheat the oven to
~ 180°C/350°F/Gas 4.
Grease two 20cm/8in sandwich cake tins and line the base of each with non-stick baking paper. Melt the chocolate in a heatproof bowl over hot water. Remove from the heat.

2 Cream the butter with the
~ sugar in a mixing bowl until pale and fluffy. Beat in the egg yolks and vanilla essence. Add the chocolate and mix thoroughly.

Take your pleasure slowly by savouring every mouthful of this sensational dark chocolate gâteau topped with brandy snap frills.

3 In a clean, grease-free
~ bowl, whisk the egg whites to soft peaks, then fold them into the chocolate mixture with the ground hazelnuts, breadcrumbs and orange rind.

4 Divide the cake mixture
~ between the prepared tins and smooth the tops. Bake for 25-30 minutes, or until well risen and firm. Turn out on to wire racks.

5 Make the brandy snaps.
~ Line two baking sheets with non-stick baking paper. Heat the butter, sugar and syrup in a saucepan over a gentle heat, stirring occasionally until smooth. Remove from the heat and stir in the flour and brandy.

6 Place small spoonfuls well
~ apart on the baking sheets and bake for 10-15 minutes, until golden. Cool for a few seconds until firm enough to lift on to a wire rack.

7 Immediately pinch the
~ edges of each brandy snap to make a frilled effect. If the biscuits become too firm, pop them back into the oven for a few minutes. Leave to set.

8 Sandwich the cake layers
~ together with half the chocolate ganache, transfer to a plate and spread the remaining ganache on top.

9 Arrange the brandy snap
~ frills over the gâteau and dust with icing sugar.

COOK'S TIP

To save time, you could use ready-made brandy snaps – simply warm them for a few minutes in the oven to make them pliable enough for shaping.

STRAWBERRY CHOCOLATE VALENTINE GATEAU

Offering a slice of this voluptuous Valentine gâteau could be the start of a very special romance.

INGREDIENTS

175g/6oz/1½ cups self-raising flour

10ml/2 tsp baking powder

75ml/5 tbsp cocoa powder

115g/4oz/½ cup caster sugar

2 eggs, beaten

15ml/1 tbsp black treacle

150ml/¼ pint/⅔ cup sunflower oil

150ml/¼ pint/⅔ cup milk

For the filling

45ml/3 tbsp strawberry jam

150ml/¼ pint/⅔ cup double or whipping cream

115g/4oz strawberries, sliced

To decorate

1 quantity Chocolate Fondant

chocolate hearts

icing sugar, for dusting

⇐ SERVES 8 ⇒

2 Add the eggs, treacle, oil and milk to the well. Mix with a spoon to incorporate the dry ingredients, then beat with a hand-held electric mixer until the mixture is smooth and creamy.

3 Spoon the mixture into the prepared cake tin and spread evenly. Bake for about 45 minutes, until well risen and firm to the touch. Cool in the tin for a few minutes, then turn out on to a wire rack to cool completely.

5 Whip the cream in a bowl until it holds its shape. Stir in the strawberries, then spread over the jam. Top with the remaining cake layer.

6 Roll out the chocolate fondant and cover the cake. Decorate with chocolate hearts and dust with icing sugar.

1 Preheat the oven to 160°C/325°F/Gas 3. Grease a deep 20cm/8in heart-shaped cake tin and line the base with non-stick baking paper. Sift the flour, baking powder and cocoa into a mixing bowl. Stir in the sugar, then make a well in the centre.

4 Using a sharp knife, slice the cake neatly into two layers. Place the bottom layer on a board or plate. Spread with strawberry jam.

COOK'S TIP

Keep the fondant closely covered until you are ready to use it, as the surface dries out fairly quickly. If this happens, the smooth effect will be spoiled.

Hot Puddings

Hot chocolate puddings appeal to anyone who craves comforting food – the sweet smell of warm chocolate from a Peachy Chocolate Bake as it cooks is hard to resist, and just the sight of proper puddings like Chocolate Chip and Banana Pudding will warm a winter's day. But if you're looking for something a little special for a dinner party, offer slices of crisp, spiced Chocolate, Date and Almond Filo Coil or luscious poached pears swathed in Chocolate Fudge Blankets.

CHOCOLATE AND ORANGE SCOTCH PANCAKES

INGREDIENTS

115g/4oz/1 cup self-raising flour

30ml/2 tbsp cocoa powder

2 eggs

50g/2oz plain chocolate,
broken into squares

200ml/7fl oz/scant 1 cup milk

finely grated rind of 1 orange

30ml/2 tbsp orange juice

butter or oil for frying

60ml/4 tbsp chocolate curls,
for sprinkling

For the sauce

2 large oranges

30ml/2 tbsp unsalted butter

45ml/3 tbsp light muscovado sugar

250ml/8fl oz/1 cup crème fraîche

30ml/2 tbsp Grand Marnier
or Cointreau

chocolate curls, to decorate

~ SERVES 4 ~

Flip for these fabulous baby pancakes in a rich creamy orange liqueur sauce. Serve them straight from the pan to enjoy them at their best.

2 Mix the chocolate and
~ milk in a saucepan. Heat gently until the chocolate has melted, then beat into the batter until smooth and bubbly. Stir in the orange rind and juice.

4 Make the sauce. Grate the
~ rind of 1 orange into a bowl and set aside. Peel both oranges, taking care to remove all the pith, then slice the flesh fairly thinly.

3 Heat a large heavy-based
~ frying pan or griddle. Grease with a little butter or oil. Drop large spoonfuls of batter on to the hot surface, leaving room for spreading. Cook over a moderate heat. When the pancakes are lightly browned underneath and bubbly on top, flip them over to cook the other side. Slide on to a plate and keep hot, then make more in the same way.

5 Heat the butter and sugar
~ in a wide, shallow pan over a low heat, stirring until the sugar dissolves. Stir in the crème fraîche and heat gently.

6 Add the pancakes and
~ orange slices to the sauce, heat gently for 1-2 minutes, then spoon over the liqueur. Sprinkle with the reserved orange rind. Scatter over the chocolate curls and serve the pancakes at once.

1 Sift the flour and cocoa
~ into a bowl and make a well in the centre. Add the eggs and beat well, gradually incorporating the surrounding dry ingredients to make a smooth batter.

HOT CHOCOLATE ZABAGLIONE

> *Once you've tasted this slinky, sensuous dessert, you'll never look at cocoa in quite the same way again.*

INGREDIENTS

6 egg yolks

150g/5oz/⅔ cup caster sugar

45ml/3 tbsp cocoa powder

200ml/7fl oz/scant 1 cup Marsala

cocoa powder or icing sugar, for dusting

SERVES 6

1 Half fill a medium saucepan with water and bring to simmering point. Select a heatproof bowl which will fit over the pan, place the the egg yolks and sugar in it, and whisk until the mixture is pale and all the sugar has dissolved.

2 Add the cocoa and Marsala, then place the bowl over the simmering water. Whisk with a hand-held electric mixer until the mixture is smooth, thick and foamy.

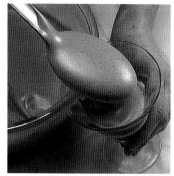

3 Pour quickly into tall heatproof glasses, dust lightly with cocoa or icing sugar and serve immediately, with Chocolate Cinnamon Tuiles or amaretti biscuits.

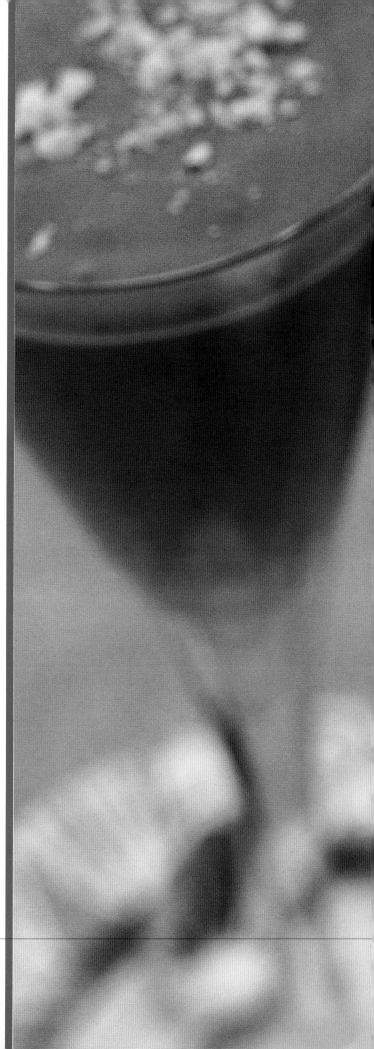

RICH CHOCOLATE BRIOCHE BAKE

This scrumptious baked dessert may be based on good old bread and butter pudding, but chocolate, brioche and bitter marmalade give it superstar status.

INGREDIENTS

200g/7oz plain chocolate, broken into squares

60ml/4 tbsp bitter marmalade

45ml/3 tbsp unsalted butter

4 individual brioches, or 1 large brioche loaf

3 eggs

300ml/½ pint/1¼ cups milk

300ml/½ pint/1¼ cups single cream

30ml/2 tbsp demerara sugar

SERVES 4

2 Melt the chocolate with the marmalade and butter in a heatproof bowl over barely simmering water, stirring the mixture occasionally.

1 Preheat the oven to 180°C/350°F/Gas 4. Lightly butter a shallow ovenproof dish.

3 Slice the brioche(s), and spread the melted chocolate mixture over the slices. Arrange them so that they overlap in the dish.

4 Beat the eggs, milk and cream in a bowl, then pour evenly over the slices. Sprinkle with the demerara sugar and bake for 40–50 minutes, until the pudding is lightly set and bubbling. Serve hot.

COOK'S TIP

Almost any bread can be used instead of brioche, except savoury varieties. Try sliced soft white rolls, currant buns or French bread for a change.

CHOCOLATE CHIP AND BANANA PUDDING

INGREDIENTS

200g/7oz/1¾ cups self-raising flour

75g/3oz/6 tbsp unsalted butter or margarine

2 ripe bananas

75g/3oz/⅓ cup caster sugar

60ml/4 tbsp milk

1 egg, beaten

60ml/4 tbsp plain chocolate chips or chopped chocolate

Glossy Chocolate Sauce, to serve

⁓ SERVES 4 ⁓

Hot and steamy, this superb light pudding has a beguiling banana and chocolate flavour.

2 Mash the bananas in a bowl. Stir them into the creamed mixture, with the caster sugar.

3 Whisk the milk with the egg in a jug or bowl, then beat into the pudding mixture. Stir in the chocolate chips or chopped chocolate.

1 Prepare a steamer or half fill a saucepan with water and bring it to the boil. Grease a 1 litre/1¾ pint/4 cup pudding basin. Sift the flour into a bowl and rub in the unsalted butter or margarine until the mixture resembles coarse breadcrumbs.

4 Spoon the mixture into the prepared basin, cover closely with a double thickness of foil, and steam for 2 hours, topping up the water as required during cooking.

5 Run a knife around the top of the pudding to loosen it, then turn it out on to a serving dish. Serve hot, with the chocolate sauce.

COOK'S TIP

If you have a food processor, make a quick-mix version by processing all the ingredients, except the chocolate, until smooth. Stir in the chocolate and proceed as in the recipe.

MAGIC CHOCOLATE MUD PUDDING

A popular favourite, which magically separates into a light and luscious sponge and a velvety chocolate sauce.

INGREDIENTS

50g/2oz/4 tbsp butter

200g/7oz/generous 1 cup light muscovado sugar

475ml/16fl oz/2 cups milk

90g/3½oz/scant 1 cup self-raising flour

5ml/1 tsp ground cinnamon

75ml/5 tbsp cocoa powder

Greek-style yogurt or vanilla ice cream, to serve

SERVES 4

1 Preheat the oven to 180°C/350°F/Gas 4. Lightly grease a 1.5 litre/2½ pint/6 cup ovenproof dish and place on a baking sheet.

2 Place the butter in a saucepan. Add 115g/4oz/¾ cup of the sugar and 150ml/¼ pint/⅔ cup of the milk. Heat gently, stirring from time to time, until the butter has melted and all the sugar has dissolved. Remove the pan from the heat.

3 Sift the flour, cinnamon and 15 ml/1 tbsp of the cocoa powder into the pan and stir into the mixture, mixing evenly. Pour the mixture into the prepared dish and level the surface.

4 Sift the remaining sugar and cocoa powder into a bowl, mix well, then sprinkle over the pudding mixture.

5 Pour the remaining milk over the pudding.

6 Bake for 45–50 minutes or until the sponge has risen to the top and is firm to the touch. Serve hot, with the yogurt or ice cream.

COOK'S TIP

A soufflé dish or similar straight-sided ovenproof dish is ideal for this, since it supports the sponge as it rises above the sauce.

CHOCOLATE CREPES WITH PLUMS AND PORT

INGREDIENTS

50g/2oz plain chocolate, broken into squares

200ml/7fl oz/scant 1 cup milk

120ml/4fl oz/½ cup single cream

30ml/2 tbsp cocoa powder

115g/4oz/1 cup plain flour

2 eggs

For the filling

500g/1¼ lb red or golden plums

50g/2oz/¼ cup caster sugar

30ml/2 tbsp water

30ml/2 tbsp port

oil, for frying

175g/6oz/¾ cup crème fraîche

For the sauce

150g/5oz plain chocolate, broken into squares

175ml/6fl oz/¾ cup double cream

30ml/2tbsp port

SERVES 6

> *A good dinner party dessert, this dish can be made in advance and always looks impressive.*

1 Place the chocolate in a saucepan with the milk. Heat gently until the chocolate has dissolved. Pour into a blender or food processor and add the cream, cocoa powder, flour and eggs. Process until smooth, then tip into a jug and chill for 30 minutes.

2 Meanwhile, make the filling. Halve and stone the plums. Place them in a saucepan and add the sugar and water. Bring to the boil, then lower the heat, cover, and simmer for about 10 minutes or until the plums are tender. Stir in the port; simmer for a further 30 seconds. Remove from the heat and keep warm.

COOK'S TIP

Vary the fruit according to what is in season, using a complementary liqueur or spirit. Try cherries with cherry brandy, mandarin orange segments with Grand Marnier or poached pears or apples with Calvados. All will taste wonderful with chocolate.

3 Have ready a sheet of non-stick baking paper. Heat a crêpe pan, grease it lightly with a little oil, then pour in just enough batter to cover the base of the pan, swirling to coat evenly. Cook until the crêpe has set, then flip it over to cook the other side. Slide the crêpe out on to the sheet of paper, then cook 9–11 more crêpes in the same way.

4 Make the sauce. Combine the chocolate and cream in a saucepan. Heat gently, stirring until smooth. Add the port and heat gently, stirring, for 1 minute.

5 Divide the plum filling between the crêpes, add a dollop of crème fraîche to each and roll them up carefully. Serve in individual bowls, with the chocolate sauce spooned over the top.

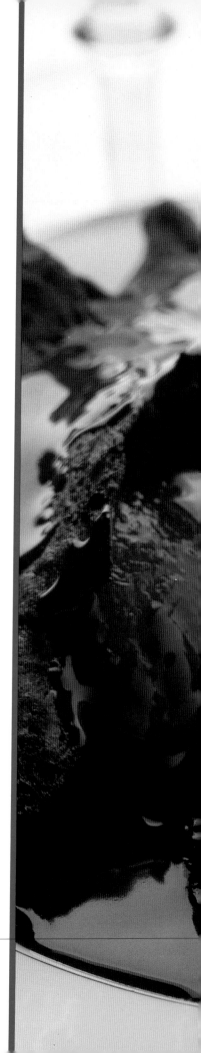

CHOCOLATE ALMOND MERINGUE PIE

> *Treat your tastebuds to the contrasting textures and flavours of fluffy meringue on a velvety smooth chocolate filling in a light orange pastry crust.*

INGREDIENTS

175g/6oz/1½ cups plain flour

50g/2oz/⅓ cup ground rice

150g/5oz/⅔ cup unsalted butter

finely grated rind of 1 orange

1 egg yolk

flaked almonds and melted plain dark chocolate, to decorate

For the filling

150g/5oz plain dark chocolate, broken into squares

50g/2oz/4 tbsp unsalted butter, softened

75g/3oz/⅓ cup caster sugar

10ml/2 tsp cornflour

4 egg yolks

75g/3oz/¾ cup ground almonds

For the meringue

3 egg whites

150g/5oz/⅔ cup caster sugar

SERVES 6

1 Sift the flour and ground rice into a bowl. Rub in the butter until the mixture resembles breadcrumbs. Stir in the orange rind. Add the egg yolk; bring the dough together. Roll out and use to line a 23cm/9in round flan tin. Chill for 30 minutes.

2 Preheat the oven to 190°C/375°F/Gas 5. Prick the pastry base all over with a fork, cover with greaseproof paper weighed down with baking beans and bake blind for 10 minutes. Remove the pastry case; take out the baking beans and paper.

3 Make the filling. Melt the chocolate in a heatproof bowl over hot water. Cream the butter with the sugar in a bowl, then beat in the cornflour and egg yolks. Fold in the almonds, then the chocolate. Spread in the pastry case. Bake for a further 10 minutes.

4 Make the meringue. Whisk the egg whites in a clean, grease-free bowl until stiff, then gradually whisk in about half the caster sugar. Fold in the remaining sugar.

5 Spoon the meringue over the chocolate filling, lifting it up with the back of the spoon to form peaks. Reduce the oven temperature to 180°C/350°F/Gas 4 and bake the pie for 15-20 minutes or until the topping is pale gold. Serve warm, scattered with almonds and drizzled with melted chocolate.

COOK'S TIP

The pastry can be made in a food processor. Pulse all the ingredients in the processor for a few seconds until the pastry just binds together. If too dry, add 5–10ml/1–2 tsp water.

CHOCOLATE, DATE AND ALMOND FILO COIL

Experience the allure of the Middle East with this delectable dessert. Crisp filo pastry conceals a chocolate and rosewater filling studded with dates and almonds.

INGREDIENTS

275g/10oz packet filo pastry, thawed if frozen

50g/2oz/4 tbsp unsalted butter, melted

icing sugar, cocoa powder and ground cinnamon, for dusting

For the filling

75g/3oz/6 tbsp unsalted butter

115g/4oz plain dark chocolate, broken into squares

115g/4oz/1 cup ground almonds

115g/4oz/⅔ cup chopped dates

75g/3oz/⅔ cup icing sugar

10ml/2 tsp rosewater

2.5ml/½ tsp ground cinnamon

SERVES 6

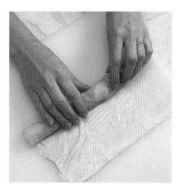

1 Preheat the oven to 180°C/350°F/Gas 4. Grease a 22cm/8½in round cake tin. Make the filling. Melt the butter with the chocolate in a heatproof bowl over barely simmering water, then remove from the heat and stir in the remaining ingredients to make a thick paste. Leave to cool.

2 Lay one sheet of filo on a clean work surface (see Cook's Tip). Brush it with melted butter, then lay a second sheet on top and brush with butter.

3 Roll a handful of the chocolate almond mixture into a long sausage shape and place along one long edge of the layered filo. Roll the pastry tightly around the filling to make a roll.

4 Place the roll around the outside of the tin. Make enough rolls to fill the tin.

5 Brush the coil with the remaining melted butter. Bake for 30–35 minutes until the pastry is golden brown and crisp. Remove the coil from the tin; place it on a plate. Serve warm, dusted with icing sugar, cocoa and cinnamon.

COOK'S TIP

Filo pastry dries out very quickly, so remove one sheet at a time and keep the rest covered with a slightly damp, clean dish towel.

PEARS IN CHOCOLATE FUDGE BLANKETS

INGREDIENTS

6 ripe eating pears

30ml/2 tbsp lemon juice

75g/3oz/⅓ cup caster sugar

300ml/½ pint/1¼ cups water

1 cinnamon stick

For the sauce

200ml/7fl oz/scant 1 cup double cream

150g/5oz/scant 1 cup light muscovado sugar

25g/1oz/2 tbsp unsalted butter

60ml/4 tbsp golden syrup

120ml/4fl oz/½ cup milk

200g/7oz plain dark chocolate, broken into squares

SERVES 6

Warm poached pears swathed in a rich chocolate fudge sauce – who could resist such a sensual pleasure?

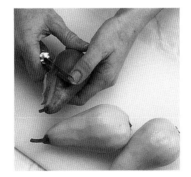

1 Peel the pears thinly, leaving the stalks on. Scoop out the cores from the base. Brush the cut surfaces with lemon juice to prevent browning.

2 Place the sugar and water in a large saucepan. Heat gently until the sugar dissolves. Add the pears and cinnamon stick with any remaining lemon juice, and, if necessary, a little more water, so that the pears are almost covered.

3 Bring to the boil, then lower the heat, cover the pan and simmer the pears gently for 15-20 minutes, or until they are just tender.

4 Meanwhile, make the sauce. Place the cream, sugar, butter, golden syrup and milk in a heavy-based saucepan. Heat gently until the sugar has dissolved and the butter and syrup have melted, then bring to the boil. Boil, stirring constantly, for about 5 minutes or until the sauce is thick and smooth. Remove from the heat and stir in the chocolate, a few squares at a time, until melted.

5 Using a slotted spoon, transfer the poached pears to a dish. Keep hot. Boil the syrup rapidly to reduce to about 45-60ml/3-4 tbsp. Remove the cinnamon stick and stir the syrup into the chocolate sauce.

6 Serve the pears in individual bowls, with the hot chocolate fudge sauce spooned over.

PEACHY CHOCOLATE BAKE

Resist everything except temptation, Oscar Wilde urged. So next time you crave something hot and chocolatey, raid the storecupboard and whip up this delicious pudding.

INGREDIENTS

200g/7oz plain dark chocolate, broken into squares

115g/4oz/½ cup unsalted butter

4 eggs, separated

115g/4oz/½ cup caster sugar

425g/15oz can peach slices, drained

SERVES 6

1 Preheat the oven to 160°C/325°F/Gas 3. Butter a wide ovenproof dish. Melt the chocolate with the butter in a heatproof bowl over barely simmering water. Remove from the heat.

2 In a bowl, whisk the egg yolks with the sugar until thick and pale. In a clean, grease-free bowl, whisk the whites until stiff.

3 Beat the chocolate into the egg yolk mixture.

4 Fold in the whites lightly and evenly.

5 Fold the peach slices into the mixture, then tip into the prepared dish.

6 Bake for 35-40 minutes, or until risen and just firm. Serve hot, with cream or yogurt if liked.

COOK'S TIP

Don't level the mixture in the dish before baking, as it looks more interesting if the surface is rough and uneven.

PRUNE BEIGNETS IN CHOCOLATE ARMAGNAC SAUCE

INGREDIENTS

75g/3oz/¾ cup plain flour

45ml/3 tbsp ground almonds

45ml/3 tbsp oil or melted butter

1 egg white

60ml/4 tbsp water

oil for deep frying

175g/6oz/¾ cup ready-to-eat stoned prunes

45ml/3 tbsp vanilla sugar

15ml/1 tbsp cocoa powder

For the sauce

200g/7oz milk chocolate, broken into squares

120ml/4fl oz/½ cup crème fraîche

30ml/2 tbsp Armagnac or brandy

SERVES 4

COOK'S TIP

Vanilla sugar is very popular in parts of Europe, where it is sold in sachets. To make your own, add a vanilla pod to a jar of caster sugar. The sugar will soon take on a subtle vanilla flavour.

Go on, indulge yourself! Slide your spoon into silky chocolate sauce, scoop up a feather-light prune beignet and get ready for rapture.

1 Start by making the sauce. Melt the chocolate in a heatproof bowl over hot water. Remove from the heat, stir in the crème fraîche until smooth, then add the Armagnac or brandy. Replace the bowl over the water (off the heat) so that it stays warm.

2 Beat the flour, almonds, oil or butter and egg white in a bowl, then beat in enough of the water to make a smooth, thick batter.

3 Heat the oil for deep frying to 180°C/350°F or until a cube of dried bread browns in 30–45 seconds. Dip the prunes into the batter and fry, a few at a time, until the beignets rise to the surface of the oil and are golden brown and crisp.

4 Remove each successive batch of beignets with a slotted spoon, drain on kitchen paper and keep hot. Mix the vanilla sugar and cocoa in a bowl or stout paper bag, add the drained beignets and toss well to coat.

5 Serve in individual bowls, with the sauce poured over the top of each serving.

HOT MOCHA RUM SOUFFLES

These superb soufflés always rise to the occasion. Serve them as soon as they are cooked for a fantastic finale to a dinner party.

INGREDIENTS

25g/1oz/2 tbsp unsalted butter, melted

65g/2½oz/generous ½ cup cocoa powder

75g/3oz/⅓ cup caster sugar

60ml/4 tbsp strong black coffee

30ml/2 tbsp dark rum

6 egg whites

icing sugar, for dusting

❧ SERVES 6 ❧

1 Preheat the oven with a ~ baking sheet inside to 190°/375°F/Gas 5. Grease six 250ml/8fl oz/1 cup soufflé dishes with melted butter.

2 Mix 15ml/1 tbsp of the ~ cocoa with 15ml/1 tbsp of the caster sugar in a bowl. Tip the mixture into each of the dishes in turn, rotating them so that they are evenly coated.

3 Mix the remaining cocoa ~ with the coffee and rum.

4 Whisk the egg whites in a ~ clean, grease-free bowl until they form firm peaks. Whisk in the remaining caster sugar. Stir a generous spoonful of the whites into the cocoa mixture to lighten it, then fold in the remaining whites.

5 Spoon the mixture into ~ the prepared dishes, smoothing the tops. Place on the hot baking sheet, and bake for 12-15 minutes or until well risen. Serve immediately, dusted with icing sugar.

COOK'S TIP

When serving the soufflés at the end of a dinner party, prepare them just before the meal is served. Pop in the oven as soon as the main course is finished and serve freshly baked.

STEAMED CHOCOLATE AND FRUIT PUDDINGS WITH CHOCOLATE SYRUP

Some things always turn out well, including these wonderful little puddings. Dark, fluffy chocolate sponge is topped with tangy cranberries and apple, and served with a honeyed chocolate syrup.

2 Peel and core the apple. Dice it into a bowl, add the cranberries and mix well. Divide among the prepared pudding basins.

3 Place the remaining muscovado sugar in a mixing bowl. Add the margarine, eggs, flour, baking powder and cocoa; beat until combined and smooth.

4 Spoon the mixture into the basins and cover each with a double thickness of foil. Steam for about 45 minutes, topping up the boiling water as required, until the puddings are well risen and firm.

5 Make the syrup. Mix the chocolate, honey, butter and vanilla essence in a small saucepan. Heat gently, stirring, until melted and smooth.

6 Run a knife around the edge of each pudding to loosen it, then turn out on to individual plates. Serve at once, with the chocolate syrup.

1 Prepare a steamer or half fill a saucepan with water and bring it to the boil. Grease four individual pudding basins and sprinkle each one with a little of the muscovado sugar to coat well all over.

COOK'S TIP

The puddings can be cooked very quickly in the microwave. Use non-metallic basins and cover with greaseproof paper instead of foil. Cook on High (100% power) for 5-6 minutes, then stand for 2-3 minutes before turning out.

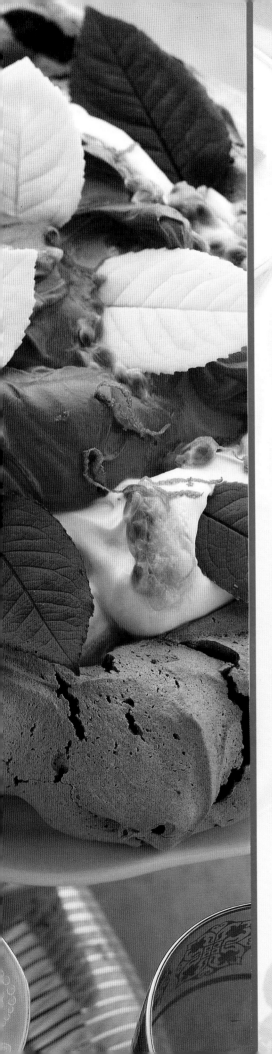

COLD DESSERTS

Cold desserts mean easy entertaining as they can mostly be prepared ahead. A rich, dark Chocolate Sorbet with Red Fruits can be made days in advance, ready to scoop and serve with fresh red fruits, or a Black and White Chocolate Mousse will keep in the fridge for the next day. But don't stop at mousses and ices — if your sweet tooth craves a really lavish treat, how about Raspberry, Mascarpone and White Chocolate Cheesecake, or, for more formal meals, an elegant Chocolate Hazelnut Galette?

BLACK AND WHITE CHOCOLATE MOUSSE

Dark and dreamy or white and creamy –
if you can't decide which mousse you
prefer, have both!

INGREDIENTS

For the White Mousse

200g/7oz white chocolate,
broken into squares

60ml/4 tbsp white rum

30ml/2 tbsp coconut cream

1 egg yolk

60ml/4 tbsp caster sugar

250ml/8fl oz/1 cup double cream

2 egg whites

For the Black Mousse

200g/7oz plain chocolate,
broken into squares

30ml/2 tbsp unsalted butter

60ml/4 tbsp dark rum

3 eggs, separated

chocolate curls, to decorate

SERVES 8

1 Make the white chocolate
~ mousse. Melt the chocolate
with the rum and coconut
cream in a heatproof bowl over
barely simmering water.
Remove from the heat.

2 Beat the egg yolk and sugar
~ in a separate bowl, then
whisk into the chocolate
mixture. Whip the cream until
it begins to hold its shape, then
carefully fold it into the
chocolate mixture.

3 Whisk the egg whites in a
~ clean, grease-free bowl
until they form soft peaks,
then fold quickly and evenly
into the chocolate mixture.
Chill until cold and set.

4 Make the dark chocolate
~ mousse. Melt the chocolate
with the butter and rum in a
heatproof bowl over barely
simmering water. Remove
from the heat and beat in the
egg yolks.

5 Whisk the egg whites to
~ soft peaks, then fold them
quickly and evenly into the
chocolate mixture. Chill until
cold and set.

6 Spoon the white and dark
~ chocolate mixtures
alternately into tall glasses or
into one large glass serving
bowl. Decorate with chocolate
curls and serve.

COOK'S TIP

Either the white or the
dark chocolate mousse
can be served alone:
simply spoon into small
pots or ramekins and
allow to set.
Alternatively, marble
the mousses.

CHOCOLATE SORBET WITH RED FRUITS

The chill that thrills – that's chocolate sorbet. For a really fine texture, it helps to have an ice-cream maker, which churns the mixture as it freezes, but you can make it by hand quite easily.

INGREDIENTS

475ml/16fl oz/2 cups water

45ml/3 tbsp clear honey

115g/4oz/½ cup caster sugar

75g/3oz/¾ cup cocoa powder

50g/2oz plain dark chocolate, broken into squares

400g/14oz soft red fruits, such as raspberries, redcurrants or strawberries

SERVES 6

2 Remove from the heat, ~ add the chocolate and stir until melted. Leave until cool.

1 Place the water, honey, ~ sugar and cocoa in a saucepan. Heat gently, stirring occasionally, until the sugar has completely dissolved.

COOK'S TIP

This sorbet looks attractive if served in small oval scoops shaped with two spoons – simply scoop out the sorbet with one tablespoon, then use another to smooth it off and transfer it to the plate.

3 Tip into an ice-cream ~ maker and churn until frozen. Alternatively, pour into a container suitable for use in the freezer, freeze until slushy, whisk until smooth, then freeze again. Whisk for a second time before the mixture hardens completely.

4 Remove from the freezer ~ 10-15 minutes before serving, so that the sorbet softens slightly. Serve in scoops, with the soft fruits.

RASPBERRY, MASCARPONE AND WHITE CHOCOLATE CHEESECAKE

Raspberries and white chocolate are an irresistible combination, especially when teamed with rich mascarpone on a crunchy ginger and pecan nut base.

INGREDIENTS

50g/2oz/4 tbsp unsalted butter

225g/8oz ginger nut biscuits, crushed

50g/2oz/½ cup chopped pecan nuts or walnuts

For the filling

275g/10oz/1¼ cups mascarpone cheese

175g/6oz/¾ cup fromage frais

2 eggs, beaten

45ml/3 tbsp caster sugar

250g/9oz white chocolate, broken into squares

225g/8oz/1½ cups fresh or frozen raspberries

For the topping

115g/4oz/½ cup mascarpone cheese

75g/3oz/⅓ cup fromage frais

white chocolate curls and raspberries, to decorate

SERVES 8

1 Preheat the oven to 150°C/300°F/Gas 2. Melt the butter in a saucepan, then stir in the crushed biscuits and nuts. Press into the base of a 23cm/9in springform cake tin.

2 Make the filling. Beat the mascarpone and fromage frais in a bowl, then beat in the eggs and caster sugar until evenly mixed.

3 Melt the white chocolate gently in a heatproof bowl over hot water, then stir into the cheese mixture with the fresh or frozen raspberries.

4 Tip into the prepared tin and spread evenly, then bake for about 1 hour or until just set. Switch off the oven, but do not remove the cheesecake. Leave it until cold and completely set.

5 Remove the sides of the tin and carefully lift the cheesecake on to a serving plate. Make the topping by mixing the mascarpone and fromage frais in a bowl and spreading the mixture over the cheesecake. Decorate with chocolate curls and raspberries.

COOK'S TIP

The biscuits for the base should be crushed quite finely. This can easily be done in a food processor. Alternatively place the biscuits in a stout plastic bag and crush them with a rolling pin.

DEVILISH CHOCOLATE ROULADE

INGREDIENTS

175g/6oz plain dark chocolate, broken into squares

4 eggs, separated

115g/4oz/½ cup caster sugar

cocoa powder for dusting

For the filling

225g/8oz plain chocolate, broken into squares

45ml/3 tbsp brandy

2 eggs, separated

250g/9oz/generous 1 cup mascarpone cheese

chocolate-dipped strawberries, to decorate

SERVES 6–8

A decadent dessert for a party or a dinner à deux: the roulade can be made a day or two ahead, then filled and rolled on the day of serving.

1 Preheat the oven to 180°C/350°F/Gas 4. Grease a 33 x 23cm/13 x 9in Swiss roll tin and line with non-stick baking paper. Melt the chocolate in a heatproof bowl over hot water, then remove from the heat.

2 Whisk the egg yolks and sugar in a bowl until pale and thick, then stir in the melted chocolate evenly.

3 In a clean, grease-free bowl, whisk the egg whites to soft peaks, then fold lightly and evenly into the egg and chocolate mixture.

4 Scrape into the tin and spread to the corners. Bake for 15-20 minutes, until well risen and firm to the touch. Dust a sheet of non-stick baking paper with cocoa. Turn the sponge out on the paper, cover with a clean dish towel and leave to cool.

COOK'S TIP

Don't worry if the roulade cracks – it's meant to!

5 Make the filling. Melt the chocolate with the brandy in a heatproof bowl over hot water. Remove from the heat. Beat the egg yolks together, then beat into the chocolate mixture. In a separate bowl, whisk the whites to soft peaks, then fold them lightly and evenly into the filling.

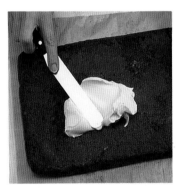

6 Uncover the roulade, remove the lining paper and spread with the mascarpone. Spread the chocolate mixture over the top, then roll up carefully from a long side to enclose the filling. Transfer to a serving plate, top with fresh chocolate-dipped strawberries and dust with cocoa powder.

Tiramisu in Chocolate Cups

Give in to the temptation of tiramisu, with its magical mocha flavour.

INGREDIENTS

1 egg yolk

30ml/2 tbsp caster sugar

2.5ml/½ tsp vanilla essence

250g/9oz/generous 1 cup mascarpone cheese

120ml/4fl oz/½ cup strong black coffee

15ml/1 tbsp cocoa powder

30ml/2 tbsp coffee liqueur

16 amaretti biscuits

cocoa powder, for dusting

For the Chocolate Cups

175g/6oz plain chocolate, broken into squares

25g/1oz/2 tbsp unsalted butter

⟨ SERVES 6 ⟩

1 Make the chocolate cups.
~ Cut out six 15cm/6in rounds of non-stick baking paper. Melt the chocolate with the butter in a heatproof bowl over barely simmering water. Stir until smooth, then spread a spoonful of the chocolate mixture over each circle, to within 2cm/¾in of the edge.

2 Carefully lift each paper
~ round and drape it over an upturned teacup or ramekin so that the edges curve into frills. Leave until completely set, then carefully lift off and peel away the paper to reveal the chocolate cups.

3 Make the filling. Beat the
~ egg yolk and sugar in a bowl until smooth, then stir in the vanilla essence and mascarpone. Mix to a smooth creamy consistency.

4 In a separate bowl, mix the
~ coffee, cocoa and liqueur. Break up the biscuits roughly, then stir into the mixture.

5 Place the chocolate cups
~ on individual plates. Divide half the biscuit mixture among them, then spoon over half the mascarpone mixture.

6 Spoon over the remaining
~ biscuit mixture (including any free liquid), top with the rest of the mascarpone mixture and dust with cocoa. Serve as soon as possible.

Cook's Tip

When spreading the chocolate for the cups, don't aim for perfectly regular edges; uneven edges will give a more frilled effect.

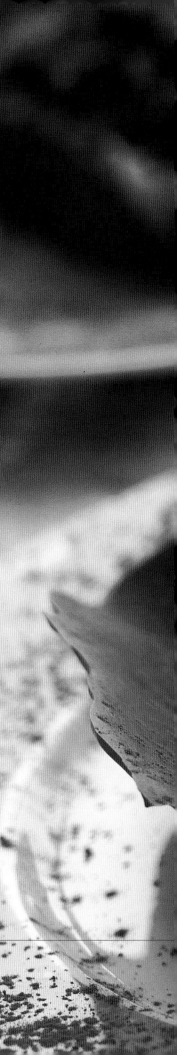

CHOCOLATE ORANGE MARQUISE

There are people who quite like chocolate, others who enjoy it now and again, and some who are utterly passionate about the stuff. If you fall into the final category, you'll adore this dense, delectable dessert.

INGREDIENTS

200g/7oz/scant 1 cup caster sugar

60ml/4 tbsp freshly squeezed orange juice

350g/12oz plain dark chocolate, broken into squares

225g/8oz/1 cup unsalted butter, cubed

5 eggs

finely grated rind of 1 orange

45ml/3 tbsp plain flour

icing sugar and finely pared strips of orange rind, to decorate

~ SERVES 6–8 ~

1 Preheat the oven to
~ 180°C/350°F/Gas 4.
Grease a 23cm/9in round cake tin with a depth of 6cm/2½in. Line the base with non-stick baking paper.

2 Place 115g/4oz/½ cup of
~ the sugar in a saucepan. Add the orange juice and stir over a gentle heat until the sugar has dissolved.

3 Remove from the heat and
~ stir in the chocolate until melted, then add the butter, cube by cube, until thoroughly melted and evenly mixed.

4 Whisk the eggs with the
~ remaining sugar in a large bowl until pale and very thick. Add the orange rind. Then, using a metal spoon, fold the chocolate mixture lightly and evenly into the egg mixture. Sift the flour over the top and fold in evenly.

5 Scrape the mixture into the
~ prepared tin. Place in a roasting tin, transfer to the oven, then pour hot water into the roasting tin to reach about halfway up the sides of the cake tin.

6 Bake for about 1 hour or
~ until the cake is firm to the touch. Remove the cake tin from the bain marie and cool for 15–20 minutes. To turn out, invert the cake on a baking sheet, place a serving plate upside down on top, then turn plate and baking sheet over together so that the cake is transferred to the plate.

7 Dust with icing sugar,
~ decorate with strips of pared orange rind and serve slightly warm or cold.

ROCKY ROAD ICE CREAM

For chills and thrills, there's nothing to beat this classic sweet ice cream packed with contrasting textures and flavours.

INGREDIENTS

115g/4oz plain chocolate, broken into squares

150ml/¼ pint/⅔ cup milk

300ml/½ pint/1¼ cups double cream

115g/4oz/1½ cups marshmallows, chopped

50g/2oz/½ cup glacé cherries, chopped

50g/2oz/½ cup crumbled shortbread biscuits

30ml/2 tbsp chopped walnuts

SERVES 6

4 Stir the marshmallows, cherries, crushed biscuits and nuts into the iced mixture, then return to the freezer container and freeze until firm.

5 Allow the ice cream to soften at room temperature for 15–20 minutes before serving in scoops.

2 Whip the cream in a bowl until it just holds its shape. Beat in the chocolate mixture.

1 Melt the chocolate in the milk in a saucepan over a gentle heat, stirring from time to time. Leave to cool completely.

3 Tip the mixture into an ice cream maker and churn until thick and almost frozen. Alternatively, pour into a container suitable for use in the freezer, freeze until ice crystals form around the edges, then whisk until smooth.

COOK'S TIP

For a quick version, simply stir the flavourings into bought soft-scoop chocolate ice cream and freeze until firm.

CHOCOLATE CONES WITH APRICOT SAUCE

INGREDIENTS

250g/9oz plain dark chocolate, broken into squares

350g/12oz/1½ cups ricotta cheese

45ml/3 tbsp double cream

30ml/2 tbsp brandy

30ml/2 tbsp icing sugar

finely grated rind of 1 lemon

strips of lemon rind, to decorate

For the sauce

175g/6oz/⅔ cup apricot jam

45ml/3 tbsp lemon juice

⁓ SERVES 6 ⁓

The seductive liaison of dark chocolate wrapped around a creamy brandy-flavoured filling makes a dramatic and delicious dessert. The cones can be made, filled and arranged with the sauce on plates before you start your meal, then chilled ready to serve.

1 Cut 12 x 10cm/4in double
⁓ thickness rounds from non-stick baking paper and shape each into a cone. Secure with masking tape.

2 Melt the chocolate in a
⁓ heatproof bowl over hot water, cool slightly, then spoon a little into each cone, swirling and brushing it to coat the paper in an even layer.

3 Stand each cone point
⁓ downwards in a cup or glass, to hold it straight. Leave in a cool place until the cones are completely set.

4 Make the sauce. Combine
⁓ the apricot jam and lemon juice in a small saucepan. Melt over a gentle heat, then cool.

5 Beat the ricotta, cream,
⁓ brandy and icing sugar in a bowl. Stir in the lemon rind.

6 Spoon or pipe the ricotta
⁓ mixture into the cones, then carefully peel off the baking paper.

7 Serve the cones in pairs on
⁓ individual plates, scattered with lemon rind and surrounded with the cooled apricot sauce.

COOK'S TIP

When making the paper cones, make sure there is no gap at the pointed end or the chocolate will run out when you coat them. It is best to let the chocolate cool slightly before use, so that it sets quickly.

WHITE CHOCOLATE VANILLA MOUSSE WITH DARK CHOCOLATE SAUCE

INGREDIENTS

200g/7oz white chocolate, broken into squares

2 eggs, separated

60ml/4 tbsp caster sugar

300ml/½ pint/1¼ cups double cream

1 sachet powdered gelatine

150ml/5fl oz/⅔ cup Greek-style yogurt

10ml/2 tsp vanilla essence

For the sauce

50g/2oz plain chocolate, broken into squares

30ml/2 tbsp dark rum

60ml/4 tbsp single cream

SERVES 6–8

COOK'S TIP

It is very important to make sure that the gelatine is completely dissolved in the cream before adding to the other ingredients. Lift a little of the mixture on a wooden spoon to check that no undissolved granules remain. Alternatively, soften the gelatine in 30ml/2 tbsp cold water in a cup, then melt it over hot water before stirring it into the heated cream.

Happy endings are assured when slices of creamy white chocolate mousse are served with a divine dark sauce.

1 Line a 1 litre/1¾ pint/ 4 cup loaf tin with non-stick baking paper or clear film. Melt the chocolate in a heatproof bowl over hot water, then remove from the heat.

2 Whisk the egg yolks and sugar in a bowl until pale and thick, then beat in the melted chocolate.

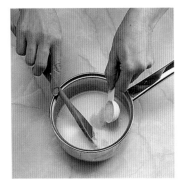

3 Heat the cream in a small saucepan until almost boiling, then remove from the heat. Sprinkle the powdered gelatine over, stirring until completely dissolved.

4 Then pour on to the chocolate mixture, whisking vigorously to mix until smooth.

5 Whisk the yogurt and vanilla essence into the mixture. In a clean, grease-free bowl, whisk the egg whites until stiff, then fold them into the mixture. Tip into the prepared loaf tin, level the surface and chill until set.

6 Make the sauce. Melt the chocolate with the rum and cream in a heatproof bowl over barely simmering water, stirring occasionally, then leave to cool completely.

7 When the mousse is set, remove it from the tin with the aid of the paper or clear film. Serve in thick slices with the cooled chocolate sauce poured around.

ITALIAN CHOCOLATE RICOTTA PIE

225g/8oz/2 cups plain flour

30ml/2 tbsp cocoa powder

60ml/4 tbsp caster sugar

115g/4oz/½ cup unsalted butter

60ml/4 tbsp dry sherry

For the filling

2 egg yolks

115g/4oz/½ cup caster sugar

500g/1¼lb/2½ cups ricotta cheese

finely grated rind of 1 lemon

90ml/6 tbsp dark chocolate chips

75ml/5 tbsp chopped mixed peel

45ml/3 tbsp chopped angelica

SERVES 6

> *This glorious pie travels well and is perfect for picnics.*

3 Make the filling. Beat the egg yolks and sugar in a bowl, then beat in the ricotta to mix thoroughly. Stir in the lemon rind, chocolate chips, mixed peel and angelica.

5 Bake for 15 minutes, then lower the oven temperature to 180°C/350°F/Gas 4 and cook for a further 30–35 minutes, until golden brown and firm. Cool in the tin.

COOK'S TIP

This pie is best served at room temperature, so if you make it in advance, chill it when cool, then bring to room temperature for about 30 minutes before serving.

1 Preheat the oven to 200°C/400°F/Gas 6. Sift the flour and cocoa into a bowl, then stir in the sugar. Rub in the butter until the mixture resembles breadcrumbs, then work in the sherry, using your fingertips, until the mixture binds to a firm dough.

2 Roll out three-quarters of the pastry on a lightly floured surface and line a 24cm/9½in loose-based flan tin.

4 Scrape the ricotta mixture into the pastry case and level the surface. Roll out the remaining pastry and cut into strips, then arrange these in a lattice over the pie.

CHOCOLATE MANDARIN TRIFLE

Trifle is always a tempting treat, but when a rich chocolate and mascarpone custard is combined with amaretto and mandarin oranges, it becomes sheer delight.

INGREDIENTS

4 trifle sponges

14 amaretti biscuits

60ml/4 tbsp Amaretto di Saronno or sweet sherry

8 mandarin oranges

For the custard

200g/7oz plain chocolate, broken into squares

30ml/2 tbsp cornflour or custard powder

30ml/2 tbsp caster sugar

2 egg yolks

200ml/7fl oz/scant 1 cup milk

250g/9oz/generous 1 cup mascarpone cheese

For the topping

250g/9oz/generous 1 cup fromage frais

chocolate shapes

mandarin slices

SERVES 6–8

1 Break up the trifle sponges and place them in a large glass serving dish. Crumble the amaretti biscuits over and then sprinkle with amaretto or sweet sherry.

2 Squeeze the juice from 2 mandarins and sprinkle into the dish. Segment the rest and put in the dish.

3 Make the custard. Melt the chocolate in a heatproof bowl over hot water. In a separate bowl, mix the cornflour or custard powder, sugar and egg yolks to a paste.

4 Heat the milk in a small saucepan until almost boiling, then pour on to the egg yolk mixture, stirring constantly. Return to the clean pan and stir over a low heat until the custard has thickened slightly and is smooth.

5 Stir in the mascarpone until melted, then add the melted chocolate, mixing it evenly. Spread evenly over the trifle, cool, then chill until set.

6 To finish, spread the fromage frais over the custard, then decorate with chocolate shapes and mandarin slices just before serving.

GREEK CHOCOLATE MOUSSE TARTLETS

INGREDIENTS

1 quantity Chocolate Shortcrust Pastry

melted dark chocolate, to decorate

For the filling

200g/7oz white chocolate,
broken into squares

120ml/4fl oz/½ cup milk

10ml/2 tsp powdered gelatine

30ml/2 tbsp caster sugar

5ml/1 tsp vanilla essence

2 eggs, separated

250g/9oz/generous 1 cup
Greek-style yogurt

SERVES 6

> *Don't be fooled by the filling – it may be based on yogurt but it's just as sinful as all the other sweet sensations in this collection!*

1 Preheat the oven to 190°C/375°F/Gas 5. Roll out the pastry and line six deep 10cm/4in loose-based flan tins.

2 Prick the base of each pastry case all over with a fork, cover with greaseproof paper weighed down with baking beans and bake blind for 10 minutes. Remove the baking beans and paper, return to the oven and bake a further 15 minutes, or until the pastry is firm. Leave to cool completely in the tins.

3 Make the filling. Melt the chocolate in a heatproof bowl over hot water. Pour the milk into a saucepan, sprinkle over the powdered gelatine and heat gently, stirring, until the gelatine has dissolved completely. Remove from the heat and stir in the chocolate.

> ### COOK'S TIP
> *If you prefer, make a large tart instead of individual ones – use a 23cm/9in flan tin.*

4 Whisk the sugar, vanilla essence and egg yolks in a large bowl, then beat in the chocolate mixture. Beat in the yogurt until evenly mixed.

5 Whisk the egg whites in a clean, grease-free bowl until stiff, then fold into the mixture. Divide among the pastry cases and leave to set.

6 Drizzle the melted chocolate over the tartlets to decorate.

CHOCOLATE AND CHESTNUT POTS

INGREDIENTS

250g/9oz plain chocolate

60ml/4 tbsp Madeira

25g/1oz/2 tbsp butter, diced

2 eggs, separated

225g/8oz/1 cup unsweetened chestnut purée

crème fraîche or whipped double cream, to decorate

☞ SERVES 6 ☜

These rich little pots, prepared in advance, are the perfect ending for a dinner party. For the very best flavour, remove them from the fridge about 30 minutes before serving, to allow them to "ripen".

1 Make a few chocolate curls for decoration, then break the rest of the chocolate into squares and melt it with the Madeira in a saucepan over a gentle heat. Remove from the heat and add the butter, a few pieces at a time, stirring until melted and smooth.

COOK'S TIP

If Madeira is not available, use brandy or rum instead. These chocolate pots can be frozen successfully for up to 2 months.

2 Beat the egg yolks quickly into the mixture, then beat in the chestnut purée, mixing until smooth.

3 Whisk the egg whites in a clean, grease-free bowl until stiff. Stir about 15ml/ 1 tbsp of the whites into the chestnut mixture to lighten it, then fold in the rest evenly.

4 Spoon the mixture into six small ramekin dishes and chill until set. Serve the pots topped with a generous spoonful of crème fraîche or whipped double cream. Decorate with the plain chocolate curls.

CHOCOLATE, BANANA AND TOFFEE PIE

Chocoholics love finding new ways of using their favourite ingredient. Here's how it can help to make the famous Banoffee Pie even more delicious.

INGREDIENTS

65g/2½oz/5 tbsp unsalted butter

250g/9oz milk chocolate digestive biscuits

chocolate curls, to decorate

For the filling

397g/13oz can condensed milk

150g/5oz plain chocolate, broken into squares

120ml/4fl oz/½ cup crème fraîche or single cream

15ml/1 tbsp golden syrup

For the topping

2 bananas

250ml/8fl oz/1 cup crème fraîche

10ml/2 tbsp strong black coffee

SERVES 6

2 Make the filling. Place the unopened can of condensed milk in a saucepan of boiling water and cover with a lid. Lower the heat and simmer for 2 hours, topping up the water as necessary. Do not allow to boil dry.

3 Remove the pan from the heat and set aside, covered, until the can has cooled down completely in the water. Do not attempt to open the can until it is completely cold, as the contents will be under pressure due to the heat.

4 Melt the chocolate with the crème fraîche or single cream and golden syrup in a heatproof bowl over barely simmering water. Stir in the caramelized condensed milk and beat until evenly mixed, then spread the filling over the biscuit crust.

1 Melt the unsalted butter in a saucepan. Crush the biscuits quite finely in a food processor or with a rolling pin. Place them in a bowl and stir in the hot melted butter. Press on to the base and sides of a 23cm/9in loose-based flan tin. Leave to set.

5 Slice the bananas and arrange them over the chocolate filling.

6 Stir together the crème fraîche and coffee, then spoon over the bananas. Decorate liberally with the chocolate curls.

GREEK CHOCOLATE MOUSSE TARTLETS

1 quantity Chocolate Shortcrust Pastry

melted dark chocolate, to decorate

For the filling

200g/7oz white chocolate,
broken into squares

120ml/4fl oz/½ cup milk

10ml/2 tsp powdered gelatine

30ml/2 tbsp caster sugar

5ml/1 tsp vanilla essence

2 eggs, separated

250g/9oz/generous 1 cup
Greek-style yogurt

~ SERVES 6 ~

*Don't be fooled by the filling – it may
be based on yogurt but it's just as sinful
as all the other sweet sensations in
this collection!*

1 Preheat the oven to
~ 190°C/375°F/Gas 5. Roll
out the pastry and line six deep
10cm/4in loose-based flan tins.

2 Prick the base of each
~ pastry case all over with a
fork, cover with greaseproof
paper weighed down with
baking beans and bake blind
for 10 minutes. Remove the
baking beans and paper, return
to the oven and bake a further
15 minutes, or until the pastry
is firm. Leave to cool
completely in the tins.

3 Make the filling. Melt the
~ chocolate in a heatproof
bowl over hot water. Pour the
milk into a saucepan, sprinkle
over the powdered gelatine
and heat gently, stirring, until
the gelatine has dissolved
completely. Remove from the
heat and stir in the chocolate.

COOK'S TIP

*If you prefer, make a
large tart instead of
individual ones – use a
23cm/9in flan tin.*

4 Whisk the sugar, vanilla
~ essence and egg yolks in a
large bowl, then beat in the
chocolate mixture. Beat in the
yogurt until evenly mixed.

5 Whisk the egg whites in a
~ clean, grease-free bowl
until stiff, then fold into the
mixture. Divide among the
pastry cases and leave to set.

6 Drizzle the melted
~ chocolate over the tartlets
to decorate.

CHOCOLATE PAVLOVA WITH PASSION FRUIT CREAM

INGREDIENTS

4 egg whites

200g/7oz/scant 1 cup caster sugar

20ml/4 tsp cornflour

45ml/3 tbsp cocoa powder

5ml/1 tsp vinegar

chocolate leaves, to decorate

For the filling

150g/5oz plain chocolate, broken into squares

250ml/8fl oz/1 cup double cream

150g/5oz/⅔ cup Greek-style yogurt

2.5ml/½ tsp vanilla essence

4 passion fruit

☞ SERVES 6 ☜

> *Passion fruit is aptly named. Serve this superb sweet and anything could happen!*

3 Spread the mixture over the marked circle, making a slight dip in the centre. Bake for 1½-2 hours.

5 Halve all the passion fruit and scoop out the pulp. Stir half into the plain cream mixture. Carefully remove the meringue shell from the baking sheet and place it on a large serving plate. Fill with the passion fruit cream, then spoon over the chocolate mixture and the remaining passion fruit.

6 Decorate with chocolate leaves before serving.

1 Preheat the oven to 140°C/275°F/Gas 1. Cut a piece of non-stick baking paper to fit a baking sheet. Draw a 23cm/9in circle on the paper and place it upside down on the baking sheet.

2 Whisk the egg whites in a clean, grease-free bowl until stiff. Gradually whisk in the sugar and continue to whisk until the mixture is stiff again. Whisk in the cornflour, cocoa and vinegar.

4 Make the filling. Melt the chocolate in a heatproof bowl over hot water, then remove from the heat and cool slightly. In a separate bowl, whip the cream with the yogurt and vanilla essence until thick. Fold 60ml/4 tbsp into the chocolate, then set both mixtures aside.

COOK'S TIP

The meringue can be baked a day in advance if necessary, and stored in an airtight container, but do not add the filling until about an hour before serving.

MISSISSIPPI MUD PIE

Mud, mud, glorious mud – isn't that what the song says? Well, you can't get much more glorious than this!

INGREDIENTS

250g/9oz/2¼ cups plain flour

150g/5oz/⅔ cup unsalted butter

2 egg yolks

15-30ml/1-2 tbsp iced water

For the filling

3 eggs, separated

20ml/4 tsp cornflour

75g/3oz/⅓ cup golden caster sugar

400ml/14fl oz/1¾ cups milk

150g/5oz plain chocolate, broken into squares

5ml/1 tsp vanilla essence

1 sachet powdered gelatine

45ml/3 tbsp water

30ml/2 tsp dark rum

For the topping

175g/6fl oz/¾ cup double or whipping cream

chocolate curls

☞ SERVES 6–8 ☜

1 Sift the flour into a bowl and rub in the butter until the mixture resembles coarse breadcrumbs. Stir in the egg yolks with just enough iced water to bind the mixture to a soft dough. Roll out on a lightly floured surface and line a deep 23cm/9in flan tin. Chill for about 30 minutes.

2 Preheat the oven to 190°C/375°F/Gas 5. Prick the pastry case all over with a fork, cover with greaseproof paper weighed down with baking beans and bake blind for 10 minutes. Remove the baking beans and paper, return to the oven and bake for a further 10 minutes, until the pastry is crisp and golden. Cool in the tin.

3 Make the filling. Mix the egg yolks, cornflour and 30ml/2 tbsp of the sugar in a bowl. Heat the milk in a saucepan until almost boiling, then beat into the egg mixture. Return to the clean pan and stir over a low heat until the custard has thickened and is smooth. Pour half the custard into a bowl.

4 Melt the chocolate in a heatproof bowl over hot water, then stir into the custard in the bowl, with the vanilla essence. Spread in the pastry case, cover closely to prevent the formation of a skin, cool, then chill until set.

5 Sprinkle the gelatine over the water in a small bowl, leave until spongy, then place over simmering water until all the gelatine has dissolved. Stir into the remaining custard, with the rum. Whisk the egg whites in a clean, grease-free bowl until stiff peaks form, whisk in the remaining sugar, then fold quickly into the custard before it sets.

6 Spoon the mixture over the chocolate custard to cover completely. Chill until set, then remove the pie from the tin and place on a serving plate. Spread whipped cream over the top and sprinkle with chocolate curls.

Mango and Chocolate Creme Brulee

INGREDIENTS

2 ripe mangoes

300ml/½ pint/1¼ cups double cream

300ml/½ pint/1¼ cups crème fraîche

1 vanilla pod

115g/4oz plain dark chocolate,
broken into squares

4 egg yolks

15ml/1 tbsp clear honey

90ml/6 tbsp demerara sugar,
for the topping

⁓ SERVES 6 ⁓

Pure luxury – exotic fruit in a honeyed chocolate custard, topped with a crunchy coating of caramelized sugar.

1 Halve, stone and peel the
⁓ mangoes. Roughly chop
the flesh and divide it among
six individual flameproof dishes
set on a baking sheet.

2 Mix the double cream and
⁓ crème fraîche in a large
heatproof bowl and add the
vanilla pod. Place the bowl
over a saucepan of barely
simmering water and stir for
about 10 minutes. Do not let
the bowl touch the water or
the cream may overheat.

3 Remove the vanilla pod
⁓ and stir in the chocolate, a
few pieces at a time, until
melted. When the mixture is
completely smooth, remove
the bowl, but leave the pan of
water over the heat.

4 Whisk the egg yolks and
⁓ clear honey in a second
heatproof bowl, then gradually
pour in the chocolate cream,
whisking constantly. Place over
the pan of simmering water
and stir constantly until the
chocolate custard thickens
enough to coat the back of a
wooden spoon.

5 Remove from the heat and
⁓ spoon the custard over the
mangoes. Cool, then chill in
the fridge until set.

6 Preheat the grill to high.
⁓ Sprinkle 15ml/1 tbsp
demerara sugar evenly over
each dessert and spray lightly
with a little water. Grill briefly,
as close to the heat as possible,
until the sugar melts and
caramelizes. Chill again before
serving the desserts.

Cook's Tip

*The mango and chocolate
custard base can be
prepared up to two days
in advance. Make the
caramelized sugar topping
several hours before
serving so that the
desserts can be chilled.*

CHOCOLATE HAZELNUT GALETTES

There's stacks of sophistication in these triple-tiered chocolate rounds sandwiched with a light fromage frais filling.

INGREDIENTS

175g/6oz plain chocolate, broken into squares

45ml/3 tbsp single cream

30ml/2 tbsp flaked hazelnuts

115g/4oz white chocolate, broken into squares

175g/6oz/¾ cup fromage frais (8% fat)

15ml/1 tbsp dry sherry

60ml/4 tbsp finely chopped hazelnuts, toasted

physalis (Cape gooseberries), dipped in white chocolate, to decorate

~ SERVES 4 ~

1 Melt the plain chocolate in a heatproof bowl over hot water, then remove from the heat and stir in the cream.

2 Draw 12 x 7.5cm/3in circles on sheets of non-stick baking paper. Turn the paper over and spread the plain chocolate over each marked circle, covering in a thin, even layer. Scatter flaked hazelnuts over the four circles, then leave until set.

3 Melt the white chocolate in a heatproof bowl over hot water, then stir in the fromage frais and dry sherry. Fold in the chopped, toasted hazelnuts. Leave to cool until the mixture holds its shape.

4 Remove the plain chocolate rounds carefully from the paper and sandwich them together in stacks of three, spooning the white chocolate hazelnut cream between each layer and using the hazelnut-covered rounds on top. Chill before serving.

5 To serve, place the galettes on individual plates and decorate with chocolate-dipped physalis.

COOK'S TIP

The chocolate could be spread over heart shapes instead, for a special Valentine's Day dessert.

$\mathscr{S}$WEETS AND DRINKS

Chocolate truffles, nutty fudge and liqueur-spiked moulded chocs and candies are simple and rewarding to make, and, packed into pretty boxes or jars, they make wonderful gifts. For after-dinner sweet treats, Cognac and Ginger Creams or Peppermint Chocolate Sticks are so much more special than bought mints. If you prefer liquid chocolate, at the end of the day you can sink into a comfy armchair with a warming glass of Irish Chocolate Velvet or Mexican Hot Chocolate.

CHOCOLATE AND CHERRY COLETTES

INGREDIENTS

115g/4oz plain dark chocolate, broken into squares

75g/3oz white or milk chocolate, broken into squares

25g/1oz/2 tbsp unsalted butter, melted

15ml/1 tbsp Kirsch or brandy

60ml/4 tbsp double cream

18-20 maraschino cherries or liqueur-soaked cherries

milk chocolate curls, to decorate

MAKES 18-20

For a sweet surprise for a friend or lover, pack these pretty little sweets in a decorative box.

4 Top each colette with a
~ chocolate curl. Leave until set, then chill in the fridge until needed.

COOK'S TIP

If foil sweet cases are difficult to obtain, use double thickness paper sweet cases instead.

3 Place one cherry in each
~ chocolate case. Spoon the white or milk chocolate cream mixture into a piping bag fitted with a small star nozzle and pipe over the cherries mounded in a generous swirl.

1 Melt the dark chocolate in
~ a bowl over hot water, then remove from the heat. Spoon into 18-20 foil sweet cases, spread evenly up the sides with a small brush, then leave in a cool place to set.

2 Melt the white or milk
~ chocolate with the butter in a heatproof bowl over hot water. Remove from the heat and stir in the Kirsch or brandy, then the cream. Cool until the mixture is thick enough to hold its shape.

COGNAC AND GINGER CREAMS

INGREDIENTS

300g/11oz plain dark chocolate, broken into squares

45ml/3 tbsp double cream

30ml/2 tbsp cognac

15ml/1 tbsp stem ginger syrup

4 pieces stem ginger, finely chopped

crystallized ginger, to decorate

MAKES 18–20

Only you know the secret of these handsome hand-made chocolates: that the mysterious dark exterior conceals a glorious ginger and cognac cream filling.

1 Polish the insides of about 18-20 chocolate moulds with cotton wool. Melt about two-thirds of the chocolate in a heatproof bowl over hot water, then spoon a little into each mould. Reserve a little of the melted chocolate, for sealing the creams.

3 Melt the remaining chocolate, then stir in the cream, cognac, ginger syrup and stem ginger, mixing well. Spoon into the chocolate-lined moulds. Warm the reserved chocolate if necessary, then spoon a little into each mould to seal. Leave in a cool place (not the fridge) until set.

4 To remove the chocolates from the moulds, gently press them out on to a cool surface. Decorate with small pieces of crystallized ginger.

COOK'S TIP

Simple chocolate moulds can be bought in most good kitchen shops and give a highly professional finish. Polishing the moulds thoroughly with fine cotton wool results in really glossy chocolates that are relatively easy to turn out. If they do stick, put them in the fridge for a short time, then try again. Don't chill them for too long, or you may dull the surface of the chocolate.

2 Using a small brush, sweep the chocolate up the sides of the moulds to coat them evenly, then invert them on to a sheet of greaseproof paper and leave to set.

CHOCOLATE FONDANT HEARTS

Get set to impress with these luscious love tokens. If you want to be really corny, pipe both sets of initials on each one.

INGREDIENTS

60ml/4 tbsp liquid glucose

50g/2oz plain dark chocolate, broken into squares

50g/2oz white chocolate, broken into squares

1 egg white, lightly beaten

450g/1lb/3½ cups icing sugar, sifted

melted plain dark and white chocolate, to decorate

~ MAKES ABOUT 50 ~

1 Divide the glucose
~ between two heatproof bowls. Place each bowl over hot water and heat the glucose gently, then add the dark chocolate to one bowl and the white chocolate to the other. Leave until the chocolate has completely melted.

2 Remove both bowls from
~ the heat and cool slightly. Add half the egg white to each bowl, then divide the icing sugar between them, mixing to combine well.

3 Knead each mixture
~ separately with your hands until it is smooth and pliable. On a surface lightly dusted with icing sugar, roll out both mixtures separately to a thickness of about 3mm/⅛in.

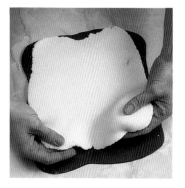

4 Brush the surface of the
~ dark chocolate fondant with egg white and place the white chocolate fondant on top. Roll the surface lightly with a rolling pin to press the pieces together.

5 Using a small heart-shaped
~ cutter, stamp out about 50 hearts from the fondant. Drizzle melted chocolate over each heart to decorate and leave until firm.

COOK'S TIP

Don't throw away the fondant trimmings – knead them together to create a marbled effect, roll the fondant out again and cut out more hearts or other shapes to use as cake decorations.

MALT WHISKY TRUFFLES

These tempting truffles make perfect presents – if you can part with them.

INGREDIENTS

200g/7oz plain dark chocolate, broken into squares

150ml/¼ pint/⅔ cup double cream

45ml/3 tbsp malt whisky

115g/4oz/1 cup icing sugar

cocoa powder, for coating

~ MAKES 25–30 ~

3 Stir in the chocolate and icing sugar, mixing evenly, then leave until firm enough to handle.

1 Melt the chocolate in a heatproof bowl over hot water, then cool slightly.

4 Dust your hands with cocoa and shape the mixture into bite-size balls. Coat in cocoa powder and pack into pretty cases or boxes. Store in the fridge for up to 3-4 days if necessary.

2 Whip the cream with the whisky in a bowl until thick enough to hold its shape.

CHOCOLATE ALMOND TORRONNE

> *Serve this speciality in thin slices.*

INGREDIENTS

115g/4oz plain dark chocolate, broken into squares

50g/2oz/4 tbsp unsalted butter

1 egg white

115g/4oz/½ cup caster sugar

50g/2oz/½ cup ground almonds

75g/3oz/½ cup chopped toasted almonds

75ml/5 tbsp chopped candied peel

For the coating

175g/6oz white chocolate, broken into squares

25g/1oz/2 tbsp unsalted butter

115g/4oz/1 cup flaked almonds, toasted

MAKES ABOUT 20 SLICES

COOK'S TIP

The mixture can be shaped into a simple round roll instead of the triangular shape if you prefer.

1 Melt the chocolate with the butter in a heatproof bowl over barely simmering water until smooth.

2 In a clean, grease-free bowl, whisk the egg white with the sugar until stiff. Gradually beat in the melted chocolate, then stir in the ground almonds, chopped toasted almonds and peel.

3 Tip the mixture on to a large sheet of non-stick baking paper and shape into a thick roll.

4 As the mixture cools, use the paper to press the roll firmly into a triangular shape. Twist the paper over the triangular roll and chill until completely set.

5 Make the coating. Melt the white chocolate with the butter in a heatproof bowl over hot water. Unwrap the chocolate roll and spread the white chocolate quickly over the surface. Press the almonds in a thin even coating over the chocolate, working quickly before the chocolate sets.

6 Chill again until firm, then cut the torronne into fairly thin slices to serve.

RICH CHOCOLATE PISTACHIO FUDGE

INGREDIENTS

250g/9oz/generous 1 cup
granulated sugar

375g/13oz can sweetened
condensed milk

50g/2oz/4 tbsp unsalted butter

5ml/1 tsp vanilla essence

115g/4oz plain dark chocolate, grated

75g/3oz/¾ cup pistachios,
almonds or hazelnuts

MAKES 36

Make a big batch of this meltingly rich chocolate fudge packed with pistachios – it won't last long!

1 Grease a 19cm/7½in square cake tin and line with non-stick baking paper. Mix the sugar, condensed milk and butter in a heavy-based pan. Heat gently, stirring occasionally, until the sugar has dissolved completely.

2 Bring the mixture to the boil, stirring occasionally, and boil until it registers 116°C/240°F on a sugar thermometer (see Cook's Tip).

3 Remove the pan from the heat and beat in the vanilla essence, chocolate and nuts. Beat vigorously until the mixture is smooth and creamy.

4 Pour the mixture into the prepared cake tin and spread evenly. Leave until just set, then mark into squares. Leave to set completely before cutting into squares and removing from the tin. Store in an airtight container in a cool place.

COOK'S TIP

If you haven't got a sugar thermometer, test the mixture by dropping a small spoonful into a cup of iced water. If you can roll the mixture to a soft ball with your fingertips, the fudge is ready.

CHOCOLATE-COATED NUT BRITTLE

Take equal amounts of pecan nuts and almonds, set them in crisp caramel, then add a dark chocolate coating for a sweet that's sensational.

INGREDIENTS

115g/4oz/1 cup mixed pecan nuts and whole almonds

115g/4oz/½ cup caster sugar

60ml/4 tbsp water

200g/7 oz plain dark chocolate, broken into squares

~ MAKES 20–24 PIECES ~

1 Lightly grease a baking
~ sheet with butter or oil.
Mix the nuts, sugar and water
in a heavy-based saucepan.
Place the pan over a gentle
heat, stirring without boiling
until the sugar has dissolved.

2 Bring to the boil, then
~ lower the heat to moderate
and cook until the mixture
turns a rich golden brown and
registers 148°C/300°F on a
sugar thermometer. To test
without a thermometer, drop a
few drops of the mixture into a
cup of iced water. The mixture
should become brittle enough
to snap with your fingers.

3 Quickly remove the pan
~ from the heat and tip the
mixture on to the prepared
baking sheet, spreading it
evenly. Leave until completely
cold and hard.

4 Break the nut brittle into
~ bite-size pieces. Melt the
chocolate in a heatproof bowl
over hot water and dip the
pieces to half-coat them. Leave
on a sheet of non-stick baking
paper to set.

COOK'S TIP

These look best in rough chunks, so don't worry if the pieces break unevenly, or if there are gaps in the chocolate coating.

PEPPERMINT CHOCOLATE STICKS

Turn the lights down low, curl up on the couch and pamper yourself with these delicious bite-size chocolate sticks.

INGREDIENTS

115g/4oz/½ cup granulated sugar

150ml/¼ pint/⅔ cup water

2.5ml/½ tsp peppermint essence

200g/7oz plain dark chocolate, broken into squares

60ml/4 tbsp toasted desiccated coconut

MAKES ABOUT 80

1 Lightly oil a large baking sheet. Place the sugar and water in a small, heavy-based saucepan and heat gently, stirring occasionally, until the sugar has dissolved completely.

2 Bring to the boil and boil rapidly without stirring until the syrup registers 137°C/280°F on a sugar thermometer. Remove the pan from the heat and add the peppermint essence, then pour on to the greased baking sheet and leave until set and completely cold.

3 Break up the peppermint mixture into a small bowl and use the end of a rolling pin to crush it into small pieces.

4 Melt the chocolate in a heatproof bowl over hot water. Remove from the heat and stir in the mint pieces and desiccated coconut.

5 Lay a 30 x 25cm/12 x 10in sheet of non-stick baking paper on a flat surface. Spread the chocolate mixture over the paper, leaving a narrow border all around, to make a rectangle measuring about 25 x 20cm/ 10 x 8in. Leave to set. When firm, use a sharp knife to cut into thin sticks, each about 6cm/2½in long.

COOK'S TIP

The set chocolate mixture could be cut into squares instead, to eat just as they are, or for decorating cakes and desserts.

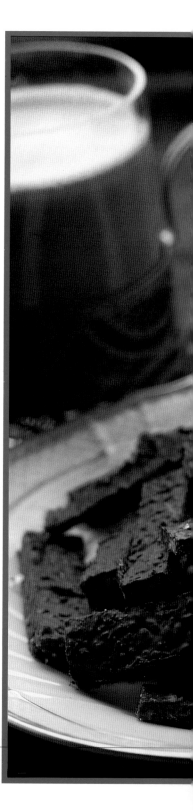

Mexican Hot Chocolate

Snuggle down in bed with a big mug of spicy hot chocolate. In Mexico, this drink is traditionally whisked with a carved wooden beater called a molinillo, but a modern blender works just as well.

INGREDIENTS

1 litre/1¾ pints/4 cups milk

1 cinnamon stick

2 whole cloves

115g/4oz plain dark chocolate, broken into squares

2-3 drops of almond essence

~ SERVES 4 ~

1 Heat the milk gently with the spices in a saucepan until almost boiling, then stir in the plain chocolate over a moderate heat until melted.

2 Strain into a blender, add the almond essence and whizz on high speed for about 30 seconds until frothy. Alternatively, whisk the mixture with a hand-held electric mixer or wire whisk.

3 Pour into heatproof glasses and serve immediately.

COOK'S TIP

If you don't have whole cinnamon and cloves, add a pinch of each of the ground spices to the mixture before whisking.

IRISH CHOCOLATE VELVET

Warm the cockles of your heart with this smooth, sophisticated drink.

INGREDIENTS

120ml/4fl oz/½ cup double cream

400ml/14fl oz/1¾ cups milk

115g/4 oz milk chocolate, broken into squares

30ml/2 tbsp cocoa powder

60ml/4 tbsp Irish whiskey

whipped cream, for topping

chocolate curls, to decorate

SERVES 4

1 Whip the cream in a bowl until it is thick enough to hold its shape.

2 Place the milk and chocolate in a saucepan and heat gently, stirring, until the chocolate has melted.

3 Whisk in the cocoa, then bring to the boil, remove from the heat and add the cream and Irish whiskey.

4 Pour quickly into four heatproof mugs or glasses and top each serving with a generous spoonful of whipped cream. Decorate with chocolate curls and serve.

COOK'S TIP

If Irish whiskey is not available, use Scotch whisky, brandy or a liqueur based on either.

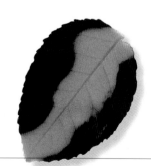

*J*CED MINT AND CHOCOLATE COOLER

> *Many chocolate drinks are warm and comforting, but this one is really refreshing — ideal for a hot summer's day.*

INGREDIENTS

60ml/4 tbsp drinking chocolate

400ml/14fl oz/1¾ cups chilled milk

150ml/5fl oz/⅔ cup natural yogurt

2.5ml/½ tsp peppermint essence

4 scoops chocolate ice cream

mint leaves and chocolate shapes, to decorate

SERVES 4

2 Pour into a cold bowl or large jug and whisk in the remaining milk, yogurt and peppermint essence.

1 Place the drinking chocolate in a small saucepan and stir in about 120ml/4fl oz/½ cup of the milk. Heat gently, stirring, until almost boiling, then remove from the heat.

3 Pour the mixture into four tall glasses and top each with a scoop of ice cream. Decorate with mint leaves and chocolate shapes. Serve immediately.

*C*OOK'S *T*IP

Use cocoa powder instead of drinking chocolate if you prefer, but add sugar to taste.

$\mathcal{B}$ASIC RECIPES

Chocolate Ganache

A luxurious, creamy frosting for gâteaux and desserts.

ENOUGH TO COVER A 23CM/9IN ROUND CAKE
250ml/8fl oz/1 cup double cream
225g/8oz plain chocolate, broken into squares

1 Heat the cream and chocolate together in a saucepan over a low heat, stirring frequently until the chocolate has melted. Pour into a bowl, leave to cool, then whisk until the mixture begins to hold its shape.

Chocolate Buttercream

A quick, everyday filling and frosting.

ENOUGH TO FILL A 20CM/8IN ROUND CAKE
75g/3oz/6 tbsp unsalted butter or margarine, softened
175g/6 oz/1½ cups icing sugar
15ml/1 tbsp cocoa powder
2.5ml/½ tsp vanilla essence

1 Place all the ingredients in a large bowl.

2 Beat well to a smooth, spreadable consistency.

White Chocolate Frosting

A fluffy, rich, white frosting for cakes and gâteaux.

ENOUGH TO COVER A 20CM/8IN ROUND CAKE
175g/6oz white chocolate, broken into squares
75g/3oz/6 tbsp unsalted butter
115g/4oz/1 cup icing sugar
90ml/6 tbsp double cream

1 Melt the chocolate with the butter in a heatproof bowl over hot water. Remove from the heat and beat in the icing sugar.

2 Whip the cream in a separate bowl until it just holds its shape, then beat into the chocolate mixture. Allow the mixture to cool, stirring occasionally, until it begins to hold its shape. Use immediately.

$\mathcal{V}$ARIATION

For a special occasion cake, stir in a tablespoon of brandy or your favourite liqueur.

Glossy Chocolate Sauce

Delicious poured over ice cream or on hot or cold desserts.

SERVES 6
115g/4oz/½ cup caster sugar
60ml/4 tbsp water
175g/6oz plain chocolate, broken into squares
30ml/2 tbsp unsalted butter
30ml/2 tbsp brandy or orange juice

1 Place the sugar and water in a saucepan and heat gently, stirring occasionally, until the sugar has dissolved.

2 Stir in the chocolate, a few squares at a time, until melted, then add the butter in the same way. Do not allow the sauce to boil. Stir in the brandy or orange juice and serve warm.

COOK'S TIP

This sauce freezes well. Pour into a freezer-proof container, seal, label and freeze for up to 3 months. Thaw at room temperature.

Chocolate Fondant

Easily moulded, this icing gives a smooth finish to celebration cakes, and can also be made into flowers, shapes or cut-outs for decoration.

ENOUGH TO COVER AND DECORATE
A 23CM/9IN ROUND CAKE
350g/12oz plain chocolate, broken into squares
60ml/4 tbsp liquid glucose
2 egg whites
900g/2lb/7 cups icing sugar

1 Melt the chocolate with the glucose in a heatproof bowl over hot water. Stir to mix, remove from the heat and cool slightly.

2 In a clean, grease-free bowl, whisk the egg whites lightly, then stir into the chocolate mixture with about 45ml/3 tbsp of the icing sugar.

3 Using an electric mixer, gradually beat in enough of the remaining icing sugar to make a stiff paste. Wrap in clear film if not using immediately.

White Chocolate Sauce

Rich and sweet, this makes a lovely contrast to a dark, bitter chocolate mousse or pudding.

SERVES 6
150ml/¼ pint/⅔ cup double cream
150g/5oz white chocolate, broken into squares
30ml/2 tbsp brandy or Cointreau

1 Heat the cream in a saucepan over a low heat until almost boiling.

2 Stir in the chocolate, a few squares at a time, until melted and smooth. Remove from the heat and stir in the brandy or Cointreau just before serving.

𝒱ARIATIONS

WHITE MOCHA SAUCE:
Stir in 30ml/2 tbsp strong black coffee just before serving.
COCONUT CHOCOLATE
CREAM SAUCE: *Stir in 45ml/3 tbsp powdered or liquid coconut cream just before serving.*

Chocolate Shortcrust Pastry (1)

A rich, dark, chocolate-flavoured pastry for sweet flans and tarts.

115g/4oz plain chocolate, broken into squares
225g/8oz/2 cups plain flour
115g/4oz/½ cup unsalted butter
15-30ml/1-2 tbsp cold water

1 Melt the chocolate in a heatproof bowl over hot water. Allow to cool but not set.

2 Place the flour in a mixing bowl. Rub in the butter until the mixture resembles fine breadcrumbs.

3 Make a well in the centre of the mixture. Add the cooled chocolate, with just enough cold water to mix to a firm dough.

Chocolate Shortcrust Pastry (2)

An alternative sweet chocolate pastry, this time made with the addition of cocoa instead of chocolate.

175g/6oz/1½ cups plain flour
30ml/2 tbsp cocoa powder
30ml/2 tbsp icing sugar
115g/4oz/½ cup butter

1 Sift the flour, cocoa and icing sugar into a bowl.

2 Place the butter in a pan with the water and heat gently until just melted. Cool.

3 Stir into the flour to make a smooth dough. Chill until firm, then roll out and use as required.

Chocolate Baskets or Cups

These impressive baskets make pretty, edible containers for mousse or ice cream.

MAKES 6
175g/6oz plain dark, milk or white chocolate
25g/1oz/2 tbsp butter

1 Cut out six 15cm/6in rounds from non-stick baking paper.

2 Melt the chocolate with the butter in a heatproof bowl over barely simmering water. Stir until smooth. Spoon one-sixth of the chocolate over each round, using a teaspoon to spread it to within 2cm/¾in of the edge.

3 Carefully lift each covered paper round and drape it over an upturned cup or ramekin, curving the edges to create a frilled effect.

4 Leave until completely set, then carefully lift off the chocolate shape and peel away the paper.

5 For a different effect, brush the chocolate over, leaving the edges jagged.

Chocolate-dipped Fruit

Strawberries, grapes, cherries and other small fruits taste absolutely delicious when fully or partially coated in chocolate, as do mandarin segments. Fruit for dipping should be ripe but not soft, and clean and dry. Whole nuts such as almonds or brazils can also be dipped.

1 Melt the chocolate and remove from the heat. Dip the fruits or nuts fully or halfway into the chocolate and allow the excess to drip off.

2 Place on a baking sheet lined with non-stick baking paper and leave until completely set.

Chocolate Squiggles

Melt a quantity of chocolate and spread fairly thinly over a cool, smooth surface. Leave until just set, then draw a citrus zester firmly across the surface to remove curls or "squiggles" of the chocolate.

ℐNDEX

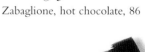